NEVER ON WEEKDAYS

Also by Henry Longhurst:

HENRY LONGHURST

Never on Weekdays

CASSELL . LONDON

CASSELL & COMPANY LTD
35 Red Lion Square, London WC1
Melbourne, Sydney, Toronto
Johannesburg, Auckland

© *Susan Jane Calver* 1968
First published 1968

S.B.N. 304 93245 0

Printed in Great Britain by
Unwin Brothers Limited
Woking and London
F. 768

CONTENTS

INTRODUCTION

On Sundays I allow myself one particular indulgence. I read bits from our four newspapers in any order I fancy. First I stare at whichever front-page headline is printed in the largest type. Then—obviously now up-to-date with current affairs—I turn to Henry Longhurst.

Why? Is it just that I like golf? Is it because he seems to share my belief not only that golf is the greatest game but also that life is golf on a smaller scale?

Perhaps it is because, before I know where I am, I seem to be taken by the ear. 'Only one man could have caught the leader,' I am reading, 'and he would have had to finish with a couple of 3s. This, at Hoylake, you simply do not get.'

Quite so, one says. Nor, really, a couple of 4s either, as Longhurst seems also to imply, although he was for many years on handicap one, if not scratch, and sometime Captain of Cambridge University golf. 'You and I,' he says—and to me personally this is rather flattering— 'would find this chip over the bunker terrifying, whereas to golfers of the Gay Brewer class . . .' It is the quiet, intimate voice, the personal approach, the voice we know so well on the TV commentaries, a hundred miles from the Gee-Whiz tone of the football reporter's professional enthusiasm. It is the voice talking to one person and that person is me. At the finish the point is tapped home with a good phrase or a quotation from the classics—P. G. Wodehouse, perhaps.

Golf is a game of character, and Longhurst describes it in terms of character. Thirty years ago he was writing of Alfred Perry's Open victory at Muirfield, and we saw it in terms of the placid simplicity of this hero, this countryman with a swing so like wielding a scythe that we 'expected him at the end of the round to take a whetstone out of his pocket'. Last year's Open was suffused with the charm of Vicenzo. In 1951 it was the character of Max Faulkner when he won at Portrush:

> As an inveterate toucher of wood and non-tempter of Fate, I can still hardly believe that the gods of golf allowed him to do so. But when he was two or three shots ahead [at the end of the *second round only*], he signed the books of the autograph hunters: 'Open Champion, 1951'.
>
> I moved silently away lest Fate mistake me for an accomplice and in some way give me the hammer, too. But he won. . . .

Great and small are given equal attention. I remember particularly the Longhurst character of Sheridan, the famous caddie-master of

Sunningdale, made clear by an analysis of the right way to 'play' him when he has told you, as always, that 'there's no caddie available, sir,' and how you must quietly assume, if you have the nerve, that a caddie will be waiting.

Besides the characters Henry Longhurst writes about, there is the character of the writer himself. A few habits and prejudices must be accepted. A certain slightly irritating gift for being in the right places at the right time. In mid-March it is no doubt his duty to be interested in a new golf course on the south coast of Spain, and one can see him, as he once described himself, sitting on a balcony in his pyjamas, the sparkling Mediterranean before him, a morning glass conceivably at his elbow, alternately writing a paragraph and then stopping to work out what day it is. He returns to favourite topics, but with a fresh approach. Match-play for ever! Stroke-play, *niet*. Now that even the US Amateur has been turned into stroke-play, 'nobody knows the name of the reigning champion'. There is an almost angry dislike of slow play, which leaves us rampageously agreeing. ('Mrs F. has taken, since her marriage to a professional, to playing at the rate of a one-legged funeral.')

There is a just perceptible dislike of innovation. At St Andrew's the University 'seems to have taken over', and to be building the 'inevitable glass boxes for training scientists prior to their emigration to the American aircraft industry'. There is a certain insistence on the regularity of course behaviour and even the fittingness of spectator apparel. On a warm day of last summer one gentleman thought it fitting to strip himself to his string vest. I only hope he did not read, on the following Sunday, the reproof administered on the back page of the *Sunday Times*.

'I sometimes wonder if Hagen would have been the same person if he had been known as Charlie Hagen instead of Walter.' If you agree with this implied conclusion, then you must also agree that 'Harry' Longhurst is equally impossible. Henry can only be Henry. And indeed the chances of there being another Henry Longhurst, another equally imperturbable Old Carthusian scratch golfer who is an adept at the Spey cast, has 'never missed a week' in his column-writing and lives in two windmills at once, are five hundred million to one against.

In my Eng. Lit. days I would have tried to place Henry in the ranks of English essayists. 'Essayist' is the wrong word for such a businesslike writer. He is far too dry for the Amontillado of Charles Lamb. He is nearer Hazlitt but won't bother so much with Lit. quotations. I would guess he often rewrites, generally with the intention of paring down. I did observe that his waste-paper basket was as big as a king-size dustbin. There is no scrap of padding in his sentences; and perhaps even the *mot juste* to him is one *mot* too many. The effect is Sheridan's 'Easy writing is damned hard reading' in reverse. But we do not read him quickly; and we are aware that we are enjoying a certain leisurely and natural warmth, and more than a little of human understanding.

9 May 1968   STEPHEN POTTER

CADDIES ANCIENT AND MODERN

As I look back on a life of golf which started when I was about ten and has taken me to many parts of the world which I otherwise would never have seen, I often think that one of its more rewarding aspects has been the association with the long and miscellaneous crew, ranging from enchanting children to out-and-out brigands, who have helped by carrying my clubs. A wonderful fellow-feeling can arise between a man and his caddie, and at its best the relationship between them can hardly, I think, be matched elsewhere in sport.

The first time I ever had my own clubs carried was during the juvenile tournament on the short course at North Foreland . . . and I doubt whether I have ever been 'closer' to a caddie since that day. His name was Frank Honour and he was on holiday from Acton. I was twelve and he, I daresay, a year or two older. He admired a pair of white shoes I was wearing, and in a burst of fellow-feeling I said that, if we won—I am sure I said 'we', not 'I'—I would give them to him. We did win and, as Endersby Howard wrote at the time, 'the tradition of kings and cobblers who were companion on the links never had happier expression'.

For my first University match, at Prince's, Sandwich, I was attended by a massive member of the Gisby family, who are well known in those parts, and I suppose he was worth at least half a dozen shots. He would point to the exact spot on which each short approach should be pitched. I soon learned to comply without argument, and would watch the ball take the slope and roll precisely round to the pin.

For two other years I had as my ally against Oxford a man who attached himself to me from Walton Heath, having sensed that the match would provide a pleasant ten days' paid holiday by the sea. At Rye all went well, though he weighed in with an observation of such calculated gamesmanship that I hesitate to repeat it,* but at Royal St George's he kept collapsing with a clatter of clubs in mid-fairway. He attributed his so constantly coming over queer to having been gassed in the First World War. Those who had been with him in the Crispin Inn overnight, however, assured me that the cause was of more recent origin, and he was replaced at the last moment by a local caddie at least as good as Gisby.

* At the 16th in the morning I was 3 up, but my opponent, Pat Jackson, was five feet away in three, while I was still off the green. At this point I holed my approach. The silence was broken by my caddie. 'Yus,' he said, 'I thought we should 'ave one of them before long.' Jackson, with whom I had been a friend and contemporary in the same house at Charterhouse, said simply, 'You little worm!'

There are of course, innumerable 'caddie stories'—indeed Charles Graves and I, before the war, published a modest anthology of them—but on looking back I find that many are inclined to be artificial. My own favourite, which sometime, somewhere, must have had a basis of truth, is of the caddie holding out an enormous divot carved up by his reverend employer. 'Shall I put this back, sir,' he is saying, 'or will you 'ave it for the 'arvest festival?'

The best, however, are liable to come, as usual, from real life. The late Tom Webster, who as a comic raconteur was almost unequalled—I was present when he actually had members of the then somewhat staid Royal Lytham and St Anne's Club rolling from their chairs—used to tell of playing at Hendon one day and remarking to his caddie on the size of the cemetery which forms the out-of-bounds for one of the longer holes.

Having announced that it was the biggest in North London, or some such, the man added with pride, 'And furthermore, sir, we have some extremely well-to-do people buried here.'

Overseas visitors to our championship courses are invariably surprised at the venerable nature of some of the caddies, and I think it is true that they go on longer here than anywhere in the world. At St Andrews some years ago, mercifully when I only had a drain-pipe bag and a few clubs, they were carried for me by an obviously senior member of the Corstophine family. When I ventured to ask his age, he revealed that he was eighty-one. He did eighteen holes in splendid style but the family, he said, would not like it if he came out again in the afternoon.

'Skip' Daniels, of Sandwich, was well into his middle sixties when he carried for Gene Sarazen, to whom he had been handed over by Walter Hagen after winning two Opens. 'He was an old boy all right, even for a professional British caddie,' Sarazen recorded later in a touching episode entitled 'My Favourite Caddie'. 'He wore a weather-beaten cap, an old celluloid collar, and a black oxford suit that had never been pressed in its lifetime. I think I fell in love with him at first sight.'

Sarazen desperately wanted to win this Open, but at the 14th at St George's, the Canal Hole, he hooked his drive and, contrary to Daniels's advice to take a mashie and make sure of a 5, he let fly impetuously with a wooden club. The ball went about thirty yards, still in the rough, and before Daniels could stop him he had chased after it and done it again. The result was a 7, and he lost the Open by those two shots. 'Before I die,' Skip said as they parted, 'I am going to win an Open championship for you.'

Four years later they were together again at Prince's, and Sarazen's story of their partnership is as moving as anything in golf. 'A terrific gale was blowing off the North Sea. As I was shaving I looked out of the window. . . . The wind was whipping the sand out of the bunkers and bending the flags. Then I saw the figure in black crouched over against the wind, pushing his way from green to green. It was Daniels, making sure of the position of the holes.'

Sarazen—and Daniels—won. And later there came an almost tearful goodbye. 'I waved to him as he pedalled happily down the drive, the coat that I had given him flapping in the breeze, and there was a good-sized lump in my throat as I thought how the old fellow had never flagged for a moment during the arduous grind of the tournament and how, pushing himself all the way, he had made good his vow to win a championship for me before he died.' They were destined never to see each other again.

THREE PENN'ORTH OF BARD

'Probably no one, not even the Bishop of St Andrews, has ever yet surmised that Shakespeare was a golfer! Proof, however, is abundant that he was not only a distinguished player acquainted with all the hazards of the game, but that he knew every peculiarity of the St Andrews links.' Such is an extract from the preface to *Shakespeare on Golf*, 24 pp., published in 1887 by David Douglas, of 15a, Castle Street, Edinburgh, at 3*d*. (by post 3½*d*.).

For myself, I am not so well acquainted as I ought to be with the writings of the Bard, whether on golf or other matters. I know, of course, of the Bishop (not, I think, of St Andrews), having taken a gigantic divot, incanting, 'O, pardon me, thou bleeding piece of earth,' and I recall Richard III's 'Put in their hands the bruising irons of wrath', and King John's more simple 'Give me the iron, I say', but the thought that there may still exist twenty-four pages of Shakespeare on golf, and particularly on the Old Course at St Andrews, is fascinating indeed.

Is it too much to hope that some reader of these notes may yet unearth a copy for me to pass on for our common enlightenment?*

The details of the book in question came from an advertisement at the back of another little book published by David Douglas called *Reminiscences of Golf on St Andrews Links* by James Balfour, who could at that time look back on forty-five years' membership of the Club.

Some of his experiences in the Club gold medal were a little unfortunate. In 1863 he seemed a certain winner. Only Robert Clark (author of the first anthology, *Golf, a Royal and Ancient Game*, in 1875) had a chance, and he was in the neighbourhood of the road at the 18th with a single shot in hand to tie. He played a long shot with his cleek and not only holed out but won the play-off.

---

* I still await a copy of *Shakespeare on Golf*, but other memorable golfing passages have in the meantime come to light. Our feelings towards the people behind who press upon us and eventually have to be let through could scarcely be better expressed than by 'Sweep on, you fat and greasy citizens!' (*As You Like It*). Falstaff's 'Three misbegotten knaves in Kendal green came at my back and let drive at me' (*cf.* Chaucer's 'Four rogues in buckram let fly at me') will also strike a chord. Again, we are always told, and truthfully enough, that no man can succeed at golf until he has mastered the art of not permitting one bad hole, or indeed one bad shot, to affect the rest of his game. The following, from *Othello*, put it better perhaps than it has ever been put before, and should be learnt by heart by all aspiring young golfers:

> To mourn a mischief that is past and gone
> Is the next way to draw new mischief on.

In another year Balfour tied with James Ogilvie Fairlie, only to have his opponent play, and win, the entire play-off without speaking. It was also at St Andrews, surely, that Bobby Jones relates having played with Harry Vardon in one of his more contemplative moods when, as he remembers, the great man uttered only once. 'Did you ever see a worse shot than that?' cried the youthful Bobby. 'No,' said Vardon.

I am grateful not only to the correspondent who sent me the book but also to another who, by coincidence, lent me on almost the same day *Some Short Stories and Sketches* by Lord Moncrieff of Tulliebole (1898), two of which also relate to golf.

If I delight in delving into the past, it is not, I like to think, because my mind dwells permanently therein, but because it proves that, despite the 7,000-yard hand-manicured courses, the gin palaces and the electric carts deemed necessary today, the original simple thrill of propelling a ball from one hole to another and, especially, the foibles, failings, and inner feelings of the golfers have remained unaltered through the years.

The scene is St Andrews and one partner in a foursome has just lit a cigar and is walking along contentedly smoking it and admiring the scenery. In what year would you say that the following was written?

'This is a fatal sign. When a man smokes, he is either winning very easily or has given up all hope; when a man draws the attention of his companions to lights and shades, and the beauty of the scenery generally, it is tantamount to his saying "as mere exercise this is a very pleasant and healthy occupation—plenty of fresh air, a charming day, and St Andrews looks very well from here; but as to its being golf, to play with a fellow who puts you into a whin or a bunker every other stroke . . .".' The answer is 1867.

Our manners on the course seem on the whole to have improved, if only for the more painful consequences of being struck by the modern ball. It is still true that golfers will 'growl and murmur if they are kept an instant waiting by the party in front and remonstrate indignantly, nay even furiously, if a ball from the party behind comes anywhere near them', but at St Andrews they cheerfully drove into the people in front, directly they had played their seconds, to 'touch them up'.

'Oh, let them out a bit, poor devils,' one character is recorded as saying, 'as though they were cheeping partridges and would not be fit for the table if taken too close.' However, the author adds, 'The most refined and effective form of cruelty is not to hit the party in front, but to keep dropping balls just behind them from a long distance. The effect on the nerves of a ball landing behind you with a thud after a flight of 150 yards, just as you are addressing your ball, will be readily understood by anyone who has endured this persecution.' It will indeed!

One thing is certain. We are more 'democratic' in our golf. 'To St Andrews,' Lord Moncrieff declares, 'where we breathe an atmosphere of pure golf, there comes occasionally some darkened man, to whom the game is unknown. If he is a distinguished stranger, pains are usually taken to enlighten him. . . . If he is an undistinguished stranger, he is, of course, tabooed at once and handed over to croquet and the ladies, if they will have him.'

We are kinder, too, to the ladies—though hardly an inch has been yielded without a struggle. At St Andrews they used to have a little course of their own, with drives limited to seventy or eighty yards—not because their ability to hit farther was doubted but because they could hardly do so without the unseemly gesture of raising the club above the shoulder. As to the real course, 'If they choose to play at times when the male golfers are feeding or resting, no one can object.'

As spectators they were regarded as the most frightful nuisance. 'If they could abstain from talking while you are playing, and if the shadow of their dresses would not flicker on the putting green while you are holing out, other objections might perhaps be waived.'

One man actually brought his wife to score for him three days running. His outraged opponent had the last word. 'Yes, my good fellow,' he said, 'but suppose we both did it.'

I am not sure whether the Prime Minister plays golf but, if so, it might well add a weapon to Mr Harold Wilson's armoury, since today presumably, as in 1890, 'there is no better preparation for the moors than golf. It hardens the muscles, both of arms and legs: and the sportsman who can take his three rounds of St Andrews links without feeling the worse for it need not be afraid of knocking up about two o'clock on the 12th of August.'*

* It was at about this time that the Conservative leader, Sir Alec Douglas-Home, was photographed during a grouse shoot and thus created the 'grouse-moor image' which was widely held to have cost the party a few million votes.

NON-CONCENTRATION CAMP

The familiar, if idiotic, adage that golf is 'ninety-per-cent mental' seems to have been lent a certain degree of truth by none other than Arnold Palmer, who the other day found himself in the strange position of being eleven strokes behind the leader. He didn't, he said, seem to be able to concentrate any more, and this in turn he attributed to the evils of giving up smoking—for which statement the cigarette manufacturers should present him with an honorarium of not less than a million dollars.

Palmer, in the days when he could keep his mind on his work, was a smoker in the twenty-per-eighteen-holes class, puffing savagely away at his cigarettes as though to ensure getting the maximum harm out of them.

He was in good company. It would have been impossible to imagine either Hogan or Hagen playing in their heyday without littering the course with half-smoked cigarettes.

For myself, after being a compulsive fifty-a-day inhaler, I am now in my eleventh smokeless month and find that I still concentrate as badly as ever. In return for a guinea towards my favourite charity I will reveal to anyone the secret of giving up smoking—unless, of course, the manufacturers care to make it worth my while not to.*

Gary Player is another who has joined the non-concentration camp—to such a degree, indeed, as to reduce his prize money, in what he describes as having been 'only a fair year', to £19,642. His trouble is sheer exhaustion, brought on by all the tournaments, exhibitions and filmed TV shows.

'Sometimes I feel so exhausted,' he is quoted as saying, 'so whipped out, so dulled that I think I can't go on, but I always do. I find myself in a daze, just playing from habit. Still,' he adds—and one can sympathize with him—'you feel that you must take advantage of all opportunities while your iron is hot.' So next year he is going to play six months and rest six months—a thought which may put ideas into the heads of us all.

I suppose there are few games in which continuous concentration is so essential as in golf, or in which it is so easy to be put off. One remembers, for instance, Mitchell Holmes, who, according to P. G. Wodehouse, 'missed short putts because of the uproar of the butter-flies in the adjoining meadows'.

There was also the character—can anyone, I wonder, tell us who it

* This brought in a great many guineas and a further article on 'How to Give Up Smoking'. One reader was so disillusioned that he actually asked for his money back.

B

actually was?—who missed one on the 6th green at Deal, which is right on the foreshore, and, raising his hands above his head, cried, 'How can anyone be expected to putt with all this bloody traffic going up and down the Channel?'

The problem of concentration in golf is a curious one and many are the ways in which people have tried to conquer it. The most complete cocoon of concentration, exceeding in its intensity even that of Hogan, was probably achieved by the late Miss Gloria Minoprio, who shook the Ladies Golf Union so rigid in 1934 by playing in the championship with one club and in trousers. It was widely—and I believe correctly—held that she played in a state of hypnosis. Certainly she gave the impression, though normally a most talented and intelligent person, of not being 'with it' while on the course.

At least one professional golfer has gained much benefit, if not from direct hypnotism, at least from 'suggestion'. I myself tried it once as a cure for twitching short putts, but it failed because the man tried to suggest something that my intellect declined to accept. All I wanted was that, the moment I stepped on to a golf green, a massive calm should come over my mind. He tried to suggest that the short putts 'would go in from now onwards'. This was manifestly beyond his terms of reference, since I might get the wrong line, or the ball hit a worm-cast, or almost anything.

Still, I should like to have another shot, and if anyone knows a good practitioner in this strange art I should be glad to know his name. I could guarantee him some pretty powerful forces to work upon.

Two of the most imperturbable golfers of all time, Walter Hagen and Bobby Locke, despite their many differences, had one common secret of success, namely that nothing in the world would induce them to hurry. Locke took the best part of an hour to get up in the morning and would spend about half an hour in the club locker-room very slowly putting on his shoes and getting ready for the fray.

Hagen of course was frequently late—not, as was sometimes suggested, in order to put the other man off, but simply because, not having got up in time, he still would not hurry.

The modern tournament golfer—and now, alas, in many cases the club golfer—is faced with a further problem, in that he has to concentrate for a longer period of time. 'If you want to have any success in America,' I remember Locke saying, 'the first thing you have to do is to learn to play slowly'—and, my word, he did!

I, on the other hand, never did, which is perhaps why I am always holding forth on the iniquities of the five-hour round—in case, like most American golfing influences, it should eventually reach us over here. For most of my life golf has been a matter of about two and a half hours, and mentally I remain a two-and-a-half-hour man. At the end of this period my thoughts stray instinctively towards the 19th.

No one who has not played in America can appreciate the anguish of mind when, the inner voice having sent up inquiries relating to the possibility of a gin and tonic, you have to reply, 'Don't be silly. We are only sitting on the 11th tee, and the four in front haven't yet driven off.' For the next two hours I find myself wandering aimlessly about the course, seeing nothing, hearing nothing, and eventually caring nothing.

Still, I am in good company. Hagen once told me how he used often to play with Babe Ruth, who was not only the world's greatest baseball player—blessed with an eye so keen he could read the title of a gramophone record while it was actually revolving—but also no mean golfer. For the first nine holes Ruth would play to professional standards, but on the way home he invariably went to pieces. The answer was that, once the normal period of a baseball game had passed, his mind went completely blank.

HIT 'EM HARDER, MATES!

Recently I wrote that it was years before there dawned on me the blindingly simple conception that it is the golfer's job to hit the ball forwards and the job of the club to hit it upwards. 'If you said,' I added, ' "A golf shot entails merely hitting a half-volley straight back to the bowler without giving a catch," everyone who has played even stump cricket would know what you meant.'

This, I am gratified to report, has drawn an unsolicited testimonial from W. J. Cox, who is renowned as one of Britain's leading teachers. He even went so far as to say it was the 'best way of putting it that he had seen for years', so we may now regard it as gospel. There will be many, no doubt, who will take from him what they wouldn't have taken from me!

Cox did, however, make an additional comment which at first surprised me. He said that practically everyone ought to hit the ball harder than they do. When you think of some of the slashing and bashing to be witnessed on any 1st tee on any Sunday morning, you would have thought the reverse to be true, but Cox, who spends a vast amount of time teaching players of every calibre, was quite firm about it.

In this he seemed to be bearing out one of the most widely quoted sayings in golf—Ted Ray's answer to a pupil who sought the secret of more length—'Hit it a——sight harder, mate.'

The attacking stroke is the one that pays off, Cox maintains. The 'nice quiet one' never pays off. He quotes that mighty hitter Harry Weetman as being quite incapable of playing a 'soft' shot, and many other pros likewise. The only thing, for instance, that has deterred David Thomas from greatness has been his fear of shots from eighty or ninety yards. He reduces championship courses to a drive and a pitch from the back tees, but from this distance there is no club with which he can hit it hard and sometimes he has been known to hit it only a few feet.

It is perhaps no coincidence that the great Arnold Palmer entitled his excellent book *Hit It Hard*. He has many times been accused, he says, of swinging so hard that his eyes bulge.

'One of the toughest plays,' he writes, 'comes when you have to choose between clubs and hit a three-quarter shot—when the distance is, say, too long for a full 9-iron and too short for a full 8-iron.' Most of us have been taught from the days of infancy that, in these circumstances, you take a 'quiet 8' and let the other man press with a 9.

This is not Palmer's view. The average player, he says, is far better of if he takes the 9-iron and hits it hard. Or, if he must take the 8,

let him hit that hard too. 'You may hit over a few greens but even this
has its good points. It builds up your ego when you overshoot the
putting surfaces and still chip back for occasional pars. You feel a lot
better than approaching the hole a foot at a time.'

Most of us, now I come to think of it, do tend to 'quit' when we try
to play anything other than a full shot, and here Palmer has a rather
good simile. 'Suppose there's a tree in front of you that won't interfere
with the flight of the ball, yet is in the way of the club's finish.
Naturally you will let up on the downswing to be sure to stop the
club before it hits the tree. Golfers who quit at contact are doing the
same thing—letting up on the downswing not on the follow-through.
. . . If you don't want to hit the ball fully, don't think about shorten-
ing the follow-through. Shorten the backswing instead.'

Cox also quoted Ben Hogan as saying that the full drive was the
easiest shot in golf, or at least relatively easy by comparison with a
holing-out putt, because it was more easy to hit straight. 'If you could
putt as straight as you drive,' added Cox, 'you would hole a hell of a
lot more putts.'

This sent me back to the days of 'equal triangles'—rather fun; try it
and see; it reminds you of when the world was young. If from 6 feet
you miss the hole by $\frac{3}{4}$ of an inch (i.e., the centre of the hole by three
inches), by how much will you miss the fairway at 250 yards? Out
with the pencil and paper!

Having carefully reduced it all to feet, I make it that X is to 750 as
$\frac{1}{4}$ is to 6. In my reckoning, which I hope will earn me '10 out of 10.v.g.',
I make X equal $31\frac{1}{4}$ feet, call it $10\frac{1}{2}$ yards. By a more complicated and
rather less confident series of calculations I make it that if you miss the
edge of the hole by 6 inches from 6 feet, as some of us may recall
from time to time having done, it is equivalent to missing the centre
of the fairway by 32 yards.

At this point those who did in fact get out their pencils and paper
in the hope of proving me wrong will now have had the pleasure of
doing so. All my sums and fractions and cancellings-out and the rest
were based on the assumption that the golf hole is $4\frac{1}{2}$ inches wide.

Instinct has just sent me to the Handbook and I find that it is in fact
$4\frac{1}{4}$. This means that you have to miss the edge by $6\frac{1}{8}$ inches instead of 6.
Never mind. In either case you are well out of bounds over the
railway line. There is only one solution, which I trust that all admirers
of these informative articles will try this weekend—and I wish I were
there to watch you. 'Hit 'em a——sight harder, mates!'

'I shall never forget my first visit to the property. . . . The long lane of magnolias through which we approached was beautiful. The old manor house with its cupola and walls of masonry two feet thick was charming. The rare trees and shurbs of the old nursery were enchanting. But when I walked out on the grass terrace under the big trees behind the house and looked down over the property the experience was unforgettable. It seemed that this land had been lying here for years just waiting for someone to lay a golf course upon it.

'Indeed, it even looked as though it were already a golf course, and I am sure that one standing today where I stood on this first visit, on the terrace overlooking the practice putting-green, sees the property almost exactly as I saw it then. The grass of the fairways and greens is greener, of course, and some of the pines are a bit larger, but the broad expanse of the main body of the property lay at my feet then just as it does now. I still like to sit on this terrace, and can do so for hours at a time. . . .'

Thus the immortal Bobby Jones, on what is now the Augusta National course in Georgia, which he and Clifford Roberts, who is still the presiding genius, founded in 1930, the year in which Jones at the age of twenty-eight retired from competitive golf having no further worlds to conquer.

As a club they wanted to create 'a retreat of such nature, and of such excellence, that men of some means and devoted to the game of golf might find the club worthwhile as an extra luxury where they might visit and play with kindred spirits from other parts of the nation'.

As to the course, they sought 'the greatest good for the greatest number'. As co-architect they incorporated Dr Alister MacKenzie. 'The doctor and I,' says Jones, 'agreed that two things were essential. First, there must be a way round for those unwilling to attempt the carry; and second, there must be a definite reward awaiting the man who makes it. Without the alternative route the situation is unfair. Without the reward it is meaningless.'

They made big, undulating greens and were, I believe, the first in America deliberately to make four different 'pin-positions'—a practice now common on nearly all new American courses of any consequence. This means that a shot good enough to stay near the flag leaves a comparatively simple putt for a birdie, while one that only finds the edge of the green leaves the player hard put to it to get down in two more. Furthermore they try to keep the pace of the greens sufficiently fast so that a well-struck shot will hold, whereas one slightly skimmed —or 'thinned', as they put it—will shoot over the back.

Four years after they started, Jones and Roberts decided to hold an invitation tournament—little knowing, I fancy, into what it was going to develop. They invited all the accepted masters of the game and almost from the beginning it became known as the Masters' tournament.

For a while they themselves decided who should be invited, but such was the immediate prestige of the tournament that a complicated system of qualification had to be devised, encompassing home and overseas players, professionals and amateurs. The sponsors nevertheless retain a power of discretion, and I suspect that anyone who started throwing clubs or tantrums in one year would not be invited the next, even if he were an Open champion.

'As far as I am concerned,' Arnold Palmer has said, 'there will never be another tournament like it.' The winner is invested with a green blazer, almost the most distinguished emblem in American golf, and becomes a member of the Masters' Club, which dines once a year, at the expense of the previous winner—on this occasion Jack Nicklaus.*

Most people, furthermore, seem to look upon the Masters as the best-run tournament in golf. 'Any club that wants to see how a tournament should be conducted should despatch a few emissaries to study the Masters,' Gene Sarazen commented fourteen years ago. 'The galleries are intelligently marshalled. The spectators as well as the golfers are treated as gentlemen. Jones will not tolerate the faintest suspicions of burlesque-show atmosphere. . . . The flavour at the Masters reflects the personality of Robert Tyre Jones, Jr, and Bob has always epitomized the best in golf.'

It was during the second Masters Tournament in 1935 that Sarazen played what might almost be described as the most historic single shot in golf. As he walked towards his second shot at the 15th—485 yards long and rated par-5—a tremendous roar from the clubhouse signified that Craig Wood had finished with a birdie 3.

Consulting with his Negro caddie, 'Stovepipe'—so called after the battered tall silk hat he always wore when caddying—Sarazen found that he needed four 3s, against a par of 5, 3, 4, 4, to win.

He decided to take a 4-wood to get the ball up and over the intervening pond and 'rode into the shot' with all his might. A moment later the spectators behind the green were jumping wildly in the air. He had holed out from 220 yards for 2! Poor Craig Wood. Sarazen tied and beat him on the play-off.

This year no fewer than five correspondents from Britain attended the Masters, and without exception they came away with the impression

* 1964.

that this was the greatest golf tournament in the world. It has everything. A course which, as set for the players, is a tremendous test of
nerve and skill; an organization second to none; provision for the
comfort and information of spectators that has grown steadily better
every year for twenty-eight years; and an atmosphere all of its own,
which has grown up perhaps through a combination of the qualities
mentioned above. It is an event which is greater than any individual
who participates in it, and the first to agree with this would be Arnold
Palmer.

The course is laid out among a combination of vast pine trees, shorter
firs, and flowering trees and shrubs, including particularly azaleas.
These are in full bloom for the tournament and the sight of the second
part of the long 13th hole will live in my memory as long as I live. The
hole is a dogleg to the left and a creek crosses the fairway and then
proceeds up the left-hand side, turns with the dogleg and runs all
alongside the second shot, finally turning again to cross directly in
front of the green and wind away round the right-hand side of it.
Meanwhile along the left of the second shot the ground rises steeply
and this bank is covered with the most magnificent orange, red and
purple azaleas, all round the foot of pine trees which must be every
inch of a hundred feet high. I spent much time there, just gazing at it
and committing it to my memory.

We were fortunate too in the weather, the best they have ever had, I
was told: four successive days of blazing sunshine that brought everything out, including the spectators, in gorgeous Technicolor. The
grass, as green as could be, is an expensive combination of basic
Bermuda, which provides an almost invisible brown and dormant
undermatting to the vivid green rye, which at this time of year
grows so fast that they have to mow it twice a day. Soon the winter
rye will die and the course will be closed until October, when it is
resown.

There is no rough on the Augusta National course, though of course
plenty of trees and sand-traps, especially round the greens. What makes
it such a tremendous test is that from the Masters tees you have to be
very long—the day of the 'good little 'un' has long since gone in
American golf—and you are then faced with the flag in any one of four
'pin-positions' on sharply sloping greens. On the final day the pins were
put in really hideously difficult positions, sometimes only four yards
from a slope rolling down into a trap, so that only a desperate man
dared 'have a go'. It is this aspect more than any other, or so I felt, that
means that no one can fluke a win in the Masters. To play at these tiny
targets knowing that you are playing for many hundreds of thousands
of dollars is a strain which anyone can understand.

The answer is that very, very few are that good, and one could see why Palmer, Nicklaus and Player are regarded in a class by themselves. In the first round Palmer and Player had 69 and Nicklaus 71. Yet they were so steady that their best ball between the three of them was only 68.

On the left of the clubhouse, as you look out towards the putting-green and the 1st and 10th tees, there is a series of white so-called 'cabins', all in the same charming Colonial architectural style as the clubhouse itself. The second on the left is Bobby Jones's, and here I was able to pay my respects again to the great man. In a prominent place on his walls are the cartoons that Tom Webster did day by day as Jones was winning his open championship at Hoylake.

The first cabin, which is in fact a most exquisite and substantial country house, was presented, anonymously, by about fifty members to General Eisenhower on his election to the Presidency in 1952. I was shown all over it by Clifford Roberts, and it did not take long to realize why, as President, Eisenhower so often managed to take both his work and his relaxation there. When his term of office came to an end, they gave him a dinner attended by those who had subscribed to the house and who thus for the first time revealed their identity.

It so happened that I was billeted in the same hospitable house during the Masters as the young South African player, Retief Waltman. I was impressed with both his golf and his attitude to life. He started the tournament with a par 72, which was highly satisfactory, but then fell back with a 77. With the course laid out as it is for the Masters, this is not a particularly bad score, but his total of 149 put him out of the running and he failed to survive what they call the 'cut'—in other words he did not qualify for the final thirty-six holes.

He thereupon handed his clubs to David Thomas and quietly, deliberately and inexorably gave up golf. It was the only grown-up life he had known. At the age of twenty-five he had already won the South African Open Championship twice, and had with great pride represented his country in the Canada Cup. It was clear that, apart from Gary Player, who did much to help him on his way, he would soon become accepted as South Africa's leading golfer. The game would give him an excellent and, one would have thought, a congenial living for the rest of his life. The whole world lay before him.

Perhaps if he had not been so good and so dedicated—his 'god' was Ben Hogan and he even wore a flat white cap in imitation of the great man—he would have settled down happily as a club professional in his native land. Ambition, however, took him farther afield and drew him into the rat-race of tournament golf. Gradually the sheer materialism of this form of life and the unceasing emphasis on money began

to sicken him, as it must have done so many before him. The difference
was that he did not threaten to give it up. He gave it up.

He came home on the second evening—I shall always remember it—
and said quietly, 'Well, I have given my clubs away and that is the
last tournament golf I shall ever play.' I seem to remember that for
good measure he had even given his golf shoes away too.

Our host and I naturally pressed him for his reasons, though neither
of us thought of trying to reconvert him to golf. He was obviously so
very sincere. He replied that, while golf had given him much, he had
never really learnt anything, and that quite simply what he wanted to
do was to 'go to school' and start again where he should never have
left off. He already had thoughts of going into the Church. Like a
surprising number of golfers, and I say it in no flippant sense, he
sincerely believed that in winning, in his own case the South African
Open, he was in receipt of divine help and guidance. Now he has
settled on the way his life shall go and he has started a two-year period
in a mission school in Pretoria, prior to entering the Church. I am sure
that everyone will join in admiration of this strength of character and
wish him well.

A SCRUFFY-LOOKING LOT

I am coming to the reluctant conclusion that golfers on the whole are a rather scruffy-looking lot. In my earlier days it used to be the custom, if memory is not deceiving me, to 'dress' for golf. Nowadays as few people seem to dress for golf as dress for dinner. They just go out in any old clothes and play—though for 'they' perhaps I should have said 'we'.

Only a few of the tournament professionals, who after all sell clothing in their shops and receive fees for endorsing golfing wear, really give a public impression of having taken trouble over their appearance. As to the average club player—well, I often wonder what visitors to our shores must think of the positively filthy collection of unwashed, long-neglected rubbish which adorns so many club locker-rooms.

I had the pleasure last week of playing in a foursome with Henry Cotton, who in a conservative way was always a 'dresser' for golf, and he echoed my sentiments with some vehemence. He was for many years attached to a shoe firm, he said, and one of his bright ideas in the cause of sales promotion was to send a man round the tournaments to clean any pair of these particular shoes that he saw in the locker-room, so that they would literally outshine their competitors on the course. In the end the man gave up. Most of the players' shoes, which they had received for nothing anyway, were already in such a state as to be not worth cleaning.

As to the trousers-tucked-into-the-socks brigade, the club secretary should be enabled, like a speed cop in America, to give them a 'ticket' on the spot—say five pounds for the first offence, ten for the second and drummed out of the club for the third. If it is muddy, what is wrong with bringing back the traditional plus-fours? And even if it is not muddy, at that. David Blair sported a splendid pair in the Walker Cup match at Seattle and with his Panama and regimental hat-band looked every inch an amateur by comparison with the rest of the team, who are now compelled to play in a uniform sort of football shirt.

Three forms of headgear receive the implacable censure of all who profess to be arbiters of golfing taste. One is that ghastly, though doubtless practical, affair that women too often wear—the one with the ear-flaps and the bits of ribbon that tie up under the chin. (What should they wear in a high wind instead? Don't ask me. I am only the critic here.)

Then for men there is the American jockey-cap, upon which it is difficult to comment in printable terms, and for some reason the white cap—except as worn by Tom Haliburton, looking as though he had just taken it from a polythene bag direct from the cleaners, as against most club golfers, whose so-called white caps look as though they had been in the bottom of the bag since Christmas. Hogan, too, is distinguishable by his flat, very white cap.

Perhaps it is an illusion that golfers were better dressed in the 'good old days'. Tomorrow, as part of the centenary celebrations at Westward Ho!, we shall have a chance of seeing, when Peter Alliss and Brian Huggett, dressed in the clothes of today, play a match against Max Faulkner and Christy O'Connor, attired as were the golfers of Westward Ho! a hundred years ago. Their apparel includes red coats, drainpipe trousers and, I trust, stiff collars. Their caddies—in real life the assistant pros from Westward Ho! and near-by Saunton—will wear long coats and bowler hats and will, of course, carry the clubs under their arms.

These clubs, some from the showcase in the club and others presented by members, will consist of a driver with a spliced-on head, a sort of spoon, a driving-iron, big mashie, mashie-niblick and putter. All the clubs, so the professional, S. Taggart, tells me, are authentic. The irons are, of course, 'old pig-iron things', not stainless steel, and there is available if necessary my favourite of all clubs, the 'rut-iron', with a face scarcely bigger than the ball.

Taggart has played with these clubs and with the gutty ball specially made by Dunlop, and says they go 'very well but not very far'. He could not, for instance, carry the big, sleepered bunker at the 4th—170 yards. At the 17th, 551 yards, his assistant was up with a drive, spoon and 9-iron. He himself was in the ditch forty yards short with three full shots.

The 'centenarians' are to receive a handicap of twelve shots. For myself I should settle for nothing short of a stroke a hole.*

* The result remains, to me, remarkable. Even if they had received a stroke a hole, I still should not, after seeing the clubs and balls and trying a swing or two wearing the clothes, have backed the Ancients against the Moderns. As it was, there was never more than one hole in it. The Moderns were 1 up after thirteen and the short 14th into the wind was halved in 3, O'Connor hitting a wonderful shot onto the green with a ninety-year-old wooden club. Faulkner holed a twenty-yarder for a net 3 at the 15th and with the Moderns making rather a mess of the 17th the Ancients were 1 up with one to play. Both their opponents easily got the 18th green but Faulkner had to play short of the ditch in two, while O'Connor, trying to get over, got in. He picked out under penalty and then, with a rusty old sharp-faced niblick, holed out from forty yards to win!

SLUGGERS' PARADISE

Throughout and after the United States Open Championship at the Country Club, Brookline, piteous cries of protest were to be heard to the effect that top-class golf was becoming a game strictly for 'muscle-men' and that the day of the true artist was done. Harrowing tales of a similar nature appear to be issuing from the Congressional Club at Washington, where this year's US Open has just been played,* and I think that, although they may not affect you and me, there is something in them.

Among the chief complainants is Jerry Barber, who captained the last American Ryder Cup team to play in this country. He is, I suppose, one of the greatest short-game players in the world—but he is also five foot five inches in height and weighs a pound or two less than ten stone.

'Golf-course architects,' he says, 'drunk with sand, length and big undulating greens, are running the little man right out of the game. They are not changing the size of tennis courts . . . and football fields are still the same, but they feel they have to make changes in golf courses. . . . Today an architect does not think he has made a good course unless at least three of the par-3s are wood shots.'

Furthermore, Barber adds, two-thirds of the par-5s have water in front of the green, so that, while the Nicklauses of this world can pitch onto the green in two, the little man has to play well short and may be faced with a hundred-yard approach instead of perhaps a thirty-yarder, from which he might well have got a 4.

Many of the courses on their tournament tour are municipal and therefore almost wholly devoid of rough. This makes them a pure sluggers' paradise and the devil take the hindmost. For the Open, however, and one or two other events, the rough is allowed to grow and courses are stretched to about 7,100 yards.

Barber quotes Oakland Hills, Detroit. 'In 1935 it was one of the finest courses I had ever played. In 1961 at the Open I hardly recognized the place. They had added more than sixty bunkers. They had made it fit the modern pattern. Everything has to be bigger and better, especially bigger.'

Billy Maxwell, Amateur Champion thirteen years ago and long a successful professional, though not a mighty hitter, blames it all on the real-estate men. Everyone wants to live beside the fairway, so on new courses you get extra-long fairways—with more building-lots to sell. 'Some of these new courses are ridiculous. They're not golf courses. They're just distance.

* 1964.

'The game itself is changing,' he adds; 'when I was growing up they would tell you not to worry about distance; just to concentrate on keeping the ball straight and in play. . . . It does not matter any more if you swing pretty, like the old Scotsmen wanted to. What matters is how far the ball goes.'

It is the custom on many American courses, understandably enough, to water a belt of the fairway at the distance from the tee at which most players' drives will finish, but there are times when the muscle-men can carry this belt and pitch on the harder ground beyond—in which case they may be as much as eighty or a hundred yards ahead.

It is no fluke that the 'big three'—Palmer, Nicklaus and Player—are big hitters; the first two mostly by nature but Player because he realized five or six years ago that he needed at least another thirty yards, or else. . . . He worked continuously on his physique for two years and then made a whole million dollars from winning the Masters.

Deane Beman, who has won the Amateur Championship on both sides of the Atlantic, is in my humble opinion every bit as good a golfer as Nicklaus, and an even better putter. Furthermore, nobody could call him a short hitter, but, unless Nicklaus plays below his best, Beman can no longer live with him.

A good example of the complete change in the problems which a championship course present to an Open Champion is afforded by a comparison between the clubs used by Willie Auchterlonie to win on the Old Course at St Andrews in 1893 and those used by Palmer at Troon in 1962.

Over the Old Course, which then measured 6,487 yards, Auchterlonie had to take a wooden club for his second at no fewer than twelve holes. There were six which he could not reach in two and at two of these he had to take the equivalent of a 4-iron for his third.

At Troon, on the other hand, which we may take to have measured a minimum of 7,000 yards, Palmer reached five greens with a drive and the smallest club in the bag, the wedge, and six more with anything from a 6-iron down to a 9. Of the two very long holes he reached one with a 3-wood and the other with a 1-iron and a very short chip.

So, while Auchterlonie took a wooden club for his second shot twelve times, Palmer needed nothing more than a 6-iron to a wedge eleven times. In between them came the great master, Harry Vardon. I did not know him well, though I did see him play, but it is my impression that this supreme golfing artist would today have been nowhere—unless, like Player, he could somehow have found an extra thirty yards.

Perhaps it does not matter what the few exceptional performers do, for what are three of them against six million of us? If it comes to that, though, we are not very good at cricket or tennis either, but it would be a poor day for us humble fry if the artistry of the great slow bowler were lost to the game because he was not a Fiery Fred and if the only man who could win at Wimbledon was the one who could serve so fast that no one could get it back.

Having put the profound problem of how to create a golf course that would give the long hitter the advantage of his length but not at the same time destroy the artist, I confess that I have no answer—unless perhaps it is the comment of Sam Snead on the layout of the Olympia Fields course near Chicago on the occasion of the PGA Championship: 'These golf architects make me sick. They can't play golf, so they try to rig the courses so nobody else can play either.'

The faintly embarrassing revelation in his speech at the prize-giving that on the previous evening he had 'got down on his knees and prayed' showed the new Open Champion,* Tony Lema, in a hitherto unsuspected light and raises a subject which must inspire in golfers a profound and, I trust, respectful interest. The possibilities it evokes are almost limitless.

The current US Open champion, Ken Venturi, said after his victory a month ago that he owed much to a long letter from his local priest, telling him among other things, 'If he asked the Lord for anything, to ask only for the faith and strength to play to the best of his ability.'

Another American, Jack Fleck, who tied for the US Open in 1955 with a rush of birdies at the end, when Hogan had already been acclaimed as the winner, and then beat the great man by three shots in a man-to-man play-off, also revealed later, in one of the magazines sponsored by that prolific evangelist Dr Norman Vincent Peale, that he had 'conquered his inner self through prayer'.

His wife, it appeared, had given him Mario Lanza's record 'I'll Walk with God', and he 'played it during the tournament whenever he needed strength'—though not, presumably, while actually on the course. We may infer that during the ensuing twelve months the record became somewhat worn, as in the next year's championship Fleck failed to qualify for the final day.

This unburdening of the heart by one of America's most respected professional golfers led to a similar reaction by an equally well known amateur, Dick Chapman, who has won the Championship on both sides of the Atlantic. His account of his experience appeared some years ago in the American magazine *Golf World*, and as a contribution to current discussion deserves a wider public.

Chapman's experience, which occurred in the final of the 1949 Canadian Amateur Championship, may be briefly summarized. In the afternoon he found himself five down with eight to play against the Canadian Phil Farley, who, having been in the final four times unsuccessfully before, was at least as anxious to win as his opponent.

'The oppressive heat and humidity,' wrote Chapman, 'were sucking my waning strength and concentration. Bad judgment and poor shots during the finishing holes were defeating me.' He therefore resorted to a constant repetition of the Lord's Prayer. Whereupon—and to

* 1964.

whom has this not at some time happened?—the still small voice of conscience said, 'If this means so much to you, you should make some sacrifice in return.'

Golf being the game it is, the elimination of bad language and profanity came at once to mind and the silent promise was accordingly made. 'It has proved,' he admitted, 'very testing on many occasions since.'

The promise having been recorded, so to speak, in the minutes, Chapman won three of the next six holes with birdies and was 2 down with two to play. His opponent duly obliged with three putts on the next and on the final hole, 225 yards against the wind, Chapman hit a 1-iron to within a few feet of the green. Farley's 4-wood faded satisfactorily towards the out of bounds on the right, only to hit a spectator on the head and bounce back into a bunker, whence he put it fifteen feet from the hole. Chapman pitched within three feet, Farley was one inch short with his putt—leaving Chapman, with what thoughts we may only surmise, an almost complete stymie.

'During the play of these last eight holes,' he wrote, 'I kept repeating the Lord's Prayer to myself. While looking at this apparently impossible situation, I observed the grain was left to right and that a cut putt might curve sharply round my opponent's ball into the cup, which is exactly what happened, to the astonishment of all.'

At long last Chapman put another 1-iron three feet from the par-5 38th hole to win with an eagle 3. 'Prayer had given me the strength, concentration and confidence necessary to perform a seemingly impossible task.'

The story is not, however, over. A dedicated golfer if ever there was one, Chapman moved straight down from New Brunswick to the New England championship where he was left to get down in two from just off the last green to win the qualifying medal. He took four more and failed even to tie. His reaction, it has to be confessed, was precisely that of the hero of P. G. Wodehouse's classic, 'Chester Forgets Himself'. '***!!!***!!!' he said, and more besides.

Suddenly the flow was interrupted by the reflection of a coin which someone had dropped on the ground. He bent to pick it up and there on the back of the coin was written—No, no. Wait for it!—the Lord's Prayer. The inscription on the other side showed that it had belonged to a stunt driver. Chapman carried it with him thereafter, including during his victory here in 1951 at Porthcawl, as an 'impressive reminder of his part of the bargain'.

Well, there we are. Theologians will be able, I am sure, to instruct us on their aspect of the matter and I shall not seek to anticipate their

C

findings. The man I am really sorry for is Farley. Five up with eight to play, he could have won peacefully by 7 and 6, had he only thought to invoke the aid of Rule 9(1)—the one about 'accepting advice or suggestion from an agency outside the match'. Penalty in match-play—loss of hole.

WANTED—A MIRACLE MAN

£3,000 per annum plus bonus is offered to leading golfer (professional or amateur), or other suitable candidate with wide knowledge of golf and experience of managing and training international sportsmen, who could select and successfully train a team of four to six tournament players. The appointment is full time and the objective is to win the British and American Open championships.

An inquiring and receptive mind, and the ability to study and improve upon existing methods, are essential. Must be a good teacher and have high qualities of leadership, perseverence and integrity. Visits to America and other overseas countries will be necessary from time to time.

Such is the, to say the least of it, unusual advertisement currently* appearing in the golfing press, and I am prepared to bet that it elicits some pretty unusual replies. Hang it, a few years ago I would have had a dart at it myself!

The originator and sponsor of this remarkable offer is Mr Ernest Butten, a management-efficiency expert, who some time ago conceived the idea of applying his professional know-how to a number of young golfers and to this end collected a stable of four. These he set to work, weight-lifting, doing press-ups and the like in a gymnasium at Sundridge Park, Kent.

Of these four, two are left to form the basis of the new squad— Jimmy McAlister (Enfield) and Tommy Horton (Ham Manor). Of the other two, one was RTU'd, as we used to say in the Army—in other words, Returned To Unit—and the other reverted voluntarily to his job as an assistant.

Mr Butten's patriotic ambitions pose several interesting problems, one of which is: 'Can golfers really be manufactured?'—by somebody else, I mean. The most successful British golfer in my lifetime—I am old enough to have seen Vardon play but not old enough to pass an opinion on his greatness—has been Henry Cotton, and here, if ever, was a manufactured player. But then he was manufactured wholly by himself.

So far as the emphasis on physical fitness is concerned, Mr Butten must assuredly be on the right lines. Golf in America, where the big money lies, is a game of endurance, in which the weak go straight to the wall. Moderate hitters are useless, however straight, and a man must be able to last out on the course for five hours or more, day

* August 1964.

after day, with a single lapse in concentration entailing the loss of thousands of dollars.

Cotton himself was a great bodybuilder, continually strengthening his left hand and his legs and hanging from horizontal bars, etcetera, and it is fair to say that it was mainly he who put into the mind of the youthful Gary Player that unless he could add thirty yards to his drive he would finish nowhere.

It is interesting to speculate on one or two Open champions past and present, as to whether they might in their formative days have emerged with success from a training establishment such as is now envisaged by Mr Butten. The 1964 Champion, Tony Lema, we may assert with some confidence, would have been RTU'd at a comparatively early stage. Gary Player on the other hand might well have adapted himself to the régime and come out top of the school. So might his young compatriot, who is now beginning to make his mark, Cobie LeGrange.

Then there are those two, so alike in name and nothing else, Hogan and Hagen. Strangely enough I believe that Hogan, if caught in his earliest days, which were pretty rough, might well have joined the school—always provided that he was aware at that time of what fantastic prizes the pinnacles of golf had to offer. If so, he would have continued hitting balls or doing extra press-ups long after the weary £3,000-a-year-and-bonus manager had gone to bed and would long since have been held up as a model for all who came after.

The very thought, however, of Hagen as a member of such an establishment—the same Hagen whose motto was 'Never hurry, never worry. Always stop and smell the flowers'—must bring a smile to all who knew him—and indeed I find myself, even as I write, unable to take the grin off my face.

Some time ago, to my great delight, a correspondent told me a new and typical 'Hagen story' relating to the famous match at Moor Park when he was beaten by Archie Compston by 18 and 17. (He went on to win the Open, of course, but that is beside the point.) The scene must, I think, have been the 15th hole, where a narrow path across the pond then forced the gallery to fall into single file. My informant was walking directly behind Hagen, who was at that time about 10 down.

Suddenly Hagen stopped dead, squatted down on his haunches, and gazed with intense interest into the water. The entire cavalcade came to a halt, like sand in a blocked egg-timer. And what was the cause of this human traffic jam? Why, Hagen had discovered some tadpoles!

Hogan, of course, would not have seen them—nor, if he had,

would he have displayed the slightest interest. But then he would not have been 10 down, either.

Everyone will wish Mr Butten and his stable well, but whether anyone, however dedicated, can become a world-class golfer operating from this country is open to doubt. I should like to see how Palmer, Nicklaus, Lema and the rest would get on in the spring, if they had lived through the winter at, say, South Herts or Hartsbourne.

Furthermore, should any of his charges rise to the top in this country for a start, he will then have to domicile them abroad, since the taxes on talent here would soon deter the most devoted golfer from the supreme extra effort needed to ascend into world class, since two-thirds of the proceeds would be destined, among other things, to help Mr Reg Maudling, the Chancellor, discover whether he could build a Channel tunnel.

The same reason will doubtless deter from applying for the job as manager the only man who could conceivably do it—namely, Henry Cotton.*

* Max Faulkner, the last British player to win the Open, took the job, but despite much enthusiasm and publicity Mr Butten's experiment faded out without proving anything one way or the other. At least one of his 'stable' may yet, however, make the grade and may look back with gratitude on those early days.

POSITIVELY NO SUBSTITUTE

I like to think that golf probably brings the fortunate camp-follower like myself into intimate contact with a greater number of truly singular characters than any other game—singular, that is, in the sense that, whatever their faults or virtues, we say of them in their lifetime 'there isn't another one exactly like him and probably never will be'.

Now it falls to me to write in the past tense of a contemporary who was unchallengeably unique—the captain-elect of the Royal St George's Golf Club, Sandwich, one with whom everyone delighted to play, not because he was 'the famous author', the man who had put the name 'James Bond' into common international speech to an extent unequalled by a fictional character since Sherlock Holmes, but simply because it was liable to be more fun playing with him than with anyone else.

No anthology of golf would be complete without at least an abbreviated version of the historic game between Bond and the infamous Goldfinger, which Ian Fleming made to take place at the club of which he was so soon to be captain, even though in the book it became the Royal St Marks and his old friend Whiting, the professional, turned into Blacking.

Incidentally, some of the golfing scenes were included in the *Goldfinger* film, but for some reason best known to themselves the makers filmed them not at St George's but at Stoke Poges, as a result of which the match never attained, to me at any rate, any sense of reality. I once asked Fleming if he minded his stories being completely altered for film purposes. 'My dear boy,' he said—and those who knew him will be able to hear him saying it—'there is nothing, absolutely nothing, about which I could care less.' I didn't believe him, then, and now, alas, never will.

I read the Goldfinger episode when it came out, but confess that I had not appreciated, till re-reading it this week, quite how true to golf it was. Psychology, gamesmanship and theory are all there, all impossible to fault. Readers of Fleming's books who are themselves familiar with any of the scenes of action will have noticed how incredibly exact an observer he was, correct in the most minute detail—yet he never seemed to take a note. I think it sprang from the fact that he was genuinely interested in people and places and so they remained in his mind.

This was certainly true of what was, so far as I know—and the more's the pity—almost his only writing about golf. Take him, for instance, on golfing attire. 'Many unlikely people play golf, including people who are blind, who have only one arm, or even no legs, and people often wear bizarre clothes to the game. Other golfers don't think them odd, for there are no rules of appearance or dress at golf. That is one of its minor pleasures. But Goldfinger had made an attempt to look smart at golf and that is the only way of dressing that is incongruous on a links.'

Who, indeed, has not seen replicas of the ghastly Goldfinger, with everything exactly right? The brilliantly polished, almost orange shoes; the plus-four suit too well cut; the plus-fours themselves pressed down the sides; the heather-mixture stockings with the green garter-tabs—and the huge black bag full of American clubs, each in its little cardboard tube, the wooden clubs hooded with leather covers bearing the name of St Marks. (However did he get into the club in the first place? one wonders—but never mind that!)

Goldfinger, I note, 'putted in the new fashion—between his legs with a mallet putter. Bond felt encouraged. He didn't believe in the system. . . .' I am sorry to see this, as the 'twitch' has just reduced me to it once again myself.

Bond himself, of course, 'knew it was no good practising. . . . His old hickory Calamity Jane had its good days and its bad. There was nothing to do about it. He knew also [a sly and not wholly unjustified dig at Royal St George's] that the St Marks practice-green bore no resemblance, in speed or texture, to the greens on the course.'

The theme of the story is that Goldfinger, the master gamesman, at crucial moments not only dropped his driver, jingled the coins in his pocket and let his shadow fall upon Bond's ball, but also improved his lie in various ways, until finally at the 17th his caddie, 'an obsequious, talkative man called Foulks,' 'found' his ball in thick rough—having actually dropped it down his trouser leg—when Bond's caddie, Hawker, with his 'keen sardonic poacher's face', had all the time got Bond's bag lying on the ground covering the real one.

All square with one to play, Bond at last 'got' his iniquitous opponent for cheating on the 18th and won his $10,000, but it was not long before a past chairman of the Rules of Golf Committee at St George's pointed out that, while Goldfinger had indisputedly cheated all the way round, he had not in fact cheated at the 18th. I will not divulge the plot in case you have not read it—but see Rule 21 (1).

Fleming was rather touchy about being thus 'caught out'—though practically nobody, myself certainly included, detected it at the time. There was, however, one other occasion on which he was taken for a minor ride on the golf course and this, I am proud to say, was by myself, on the New Course at Sunningdale. His handicap was then about eleven.

On the 1st tee he announced summarily, 'We'd better play for a couple of quid, if only to keep up the interest. I'll give you four shots.' He made a mess of the first two holes, which left me 2 up. At the short 5th I sliced into the bunker and the ball lay right at the back, on a down slope, down wind, and with a very narrow green. I splashed it nonchalantly out to within a foot of the hole, the shot of a lifetime.

'Hey!' he said sharply. 'What's your handicap?' 'Oh,' I said airily, 'I was scratch for about twenty years, but now that I hardly play I'm five.' Goldfinger, I felt, as I pocketed his two quid, would have been proud of me.

Ian Fleming used, I believe, to dine out on this little story. It seems terrible that none of us will ever dine out with him again. He was a character for whom there will be positively no substitute in our lifetime.

DELIRIOUS SUGGESTIONS

Having been taken queer almost within minutes of watching the new captain drive himself in at St Andrews, though there was, I am sure, no connection between the two events, and having then crept home only to find at Gatwick Airport not merely my temperature at 104 but also a flat tyre, I have been intermittently confined to barracks ever since and thus to my great regret missed the Ladies Championship at Prince's.

Men's amateur golf, for some reason which perhaps only sociologists could answer, seems to be losing its public appeal. Anyway, most of the 'news' in golf now concerns not amateurs—and this applies all over the world—but professionals and, in particular, how much money they win. This to the true lover of golf soon becomes monotonous, and it was against this background that I found myself recapturing all the oldtime excitement when watching the Curtis Cup match at Porthcawl. The answer is that 'given a reasonable course' the best of the women play just as well as the men, and are a good deal more decorative.

What scratch man, for instance, would have backed himself to beat Mrs Spearman or Miss Gunderson, who halved their match in 71, or to have stayed level last week with Miss Sorenson, the new Champion, and Miss White, who each went out at Prince's in 31. These girls play at a lively speed and in the best possible spirit, and, if you want to watch golf at its best, go and see the Curtis Cup match. A friend who watched them at Sandwich said that one of the American girls took a look at Prince's and said how strange it seemed. It was the only course she had ever seen, she said, where there weren't any trees. Since then I have been ranging in my mind round the many courses I have played in the United States and I cannot think of one—even Pebble Beach or Cypress Point, which are right beside the ocean—of which trees are not a leading feature.

None of what we consider our own best courses have any at all. St Andrews, Birkdale and Rye (though only at the last hole) have their own species of whins or scrub, but many, like Hoylake (though you can hook into an orchard), Prince's, St George's and Deal, where I seem to remember slicing out of bounds into a solitary and rather scruffy elderberry bush on the 12th, have no extraneous vegetation on the course at all.

Fashions in golf architecture and hazards seem to be changing, I think for the better, and the 'no-rough' school has gained great ground in America, where they tend more and more to cut the grass under the trees and let the trees make hazards on their own. In this country they learnt on the public courses at Richmond Park long before the war that the only way to get people round in reasonable time was to eliminate thick rough. I believe the suggestion came from J. H. Taylor. At any rate it worked.

The modern school of architects tends to hold that for the modest player the game itself is difficult enough, without adding sandpits to catch a bad drive, and reduce themselves to 'strategic' bunkers which govern the play of the hole for the man who can really hit the ball. Many club committees have not yet come round to this way of thinking—if indeed they have thought of it at all—but, if they did, they might find they could walk round their course and eliminate as many as a third of all the bunkers—some of which they may not remember having seen for twenty years.

The Old Course at St Andrews is thick with bunkers which absolutely govern the play of the hole, and this of course is part of its greatness, because before every shot you have to answer what the Army, I remember, used to insist upon as Paragraph 1, headed 'Object'—namely, 'What exactly is it that I am trying to do?' —and surprisingly difficult it often was to answer, at that.

One of the greatest of these strategic bunkers seems to me, with changes in balls and clubs, to be now in the wrong place, and though a lifelong adherent of the 'leave-it-alone' school regarding the Old Course, I feel, greatly daring, that it might be moved. This is the Principals' Nose, together with its attendant satellite just farther on, Deacon Sime.

Even if you do not know the Old Course, the position is easy to appreciate at the 16th, a two-shot hole of about 380 yards. You tee up beside the railway line and the fairway and the line (on the right) march side by side from tee to green. At 190 yards from the tee are the three pit-like bunkers that make up the Principal's Nose, and beyond them, invisible at about 225 yards, lurks Deacon Sime.

Though big hitters can in certain circumstances carry the lot, these bunkers normally dictate the play of the hole and originally from a shorter distance one had to decide whether to risk the right-hand line between the bunkers and the out-of-bounds railway, thus making an easier hole of it, or to turn half left, play safe and accept a much more difficult second.

The distance between bunkers and the railway is, I should say from memory, twenty paces, and at 200 yards this target simply is not 'on'. The more daring route has thus long been ruled out—'strictly for amateurs,' Von Nida called it—and the true character of the hole is lost. I should like to see the Principal's Nose and Deacon Sime measured one day to the nearest centimetre and recreated overnight fifteen yards to the left. Then once again the 16th would be one of the great two-shot holes of golf. What is more, I would move the famous Hell Bunker too—but perhaps this only proves that recent indispositions have made me delirious!

'BETTER ON ONE LEG'

I have spent much of the week among the younger generation, and a refereshing, though at times humbling, experience it has been. It seems that the human race is rapidly growing bigger. In Japan, I have read somewhere, a suit which before the war fitted a man now fits only a boy. Nearer home I had the pleasure of playing at Sunningdale in a congenial foursomes match against the boys of Eton, some of whom were a mere sixteen.

Looking back over all too many years, I see the Cambridge team, of which I had the honour to be captain, as a series of almost pygmy-like figures besides these young giants. Having reached the stage where I hit about one really good drive per round, it disconcerts me to find that a half-smothered slice by some so-called boy still leaves me due to play the second shot by about forty-five yards.

On the following day I attended the opening of the nine-hole course designed by Mr C. K. Cotton in the grounds of Stowe School and built at a cost of only £4,000, largely with the aid of boys working in their spare time and, I dare say, a few volunteers in the shape of 'you, you and you'. How lucky they are, and how times have changed since the days when golf was so foolishly frowned upon as 'a selfish game'!

To start the round at the foot of the steps of the vast mansion looking down the mile-long avenue of elms which a former Duke of Buckingham, having moved an entire village because he could see it from his window, proposed to continue in a straight line all the way to Marble Arch, is really quite an experience.

The opening was celebrated by a better-ball match between Bernard Hunt and John Jacobs on the one side and the boy champion Peter Townsend, the British girl champion Pam Tredinnick and the English girl champion Shirley Ward on the other. They played level, which I thought was a trifle hard, but not a bit of it—the young ones beat the professors by a hole, Townsend going round in 32 against Jacobs's 33 and Hunt's 34 and Miss Tredinnick contributing with a 2 at one hole.

All this was preceded on the 1st tee by what is known for want of a better word—though I live in hope that one may one day be found—as a 'clinic'. Jacobs, having explained that, however boring it might sound, you could not play golf unless you got the grip and the stance right, proved that, once you did, it was easy.

Standing on his left leg alone, he hit two perfect drives down the middle. Then, after addressing the ball, he looked Hunt in the eye and, while continuing to do so, hit a perfect couple more. This was really excellent stuff, especially when he failed to hit his opening drive in the match very well and a voice was heard to say, 'You're better on one leg.'

Before the match the girls were subjected to the ordeal of hitting demonstration shots off a somewhat downhanging lie in front of several hundred people. My heart bled for them, but it need not have done. Only one shot was slightly topped. They looked very fetching in their skiing pants, and the older boys might be forgiven if at times their attention wandered from the golf. What a long way we have come, it struck me, since the first lady turned up at the championship in trousers and the Ladies Golf Union at once slapped a notice on the board 'deploring any departure from the traditional costume of the game'.

Peter Townsend is clearly a 'prospect' of a high order and impressed me not as a person who was playing well that day but as one who was hitting the ball in a given direction because that is where he meant it to go—which is a very different thing.

Since the way is wide open for some young fellow, when the present winners begin to feel their years, to step in and make a five-figure income from golf, the thought of turning professional must always be in his mind.* If so, this is the way to do it. There is no longer any future in first being an assistant—whose job, after all, is to stay and mind the shop while the professional is earning his living outside.

On a lighter note, I cannot resist telling out of school a tale told me in school—to be precise, during lunch in the cricket pavilion—by the recently appointed headmaster of Stowe, Mr R. Q. Drayson. In the summer term, it appears, before he had come to know all the 600-odd boys, Stowe were engaged at home in a tennis match. Noting a boy with a particularly ghastly Beatle hair-style, the headmaster told him sternly to get it cut and report for inspection at 8.30 in the morning—an injunction with which I am sure the majority of our readers will be in sympathy.

Unfortunately, however, this boy was not at Stowe. He was a member of the opposition!

* He did in fact turn pro soon afterwards and, after the apparently inevitable period when he could not hit his hat, won the Dutch Open and at the moment of writing may well be set for a lucrative career.

GOLF ACROSS THE WATER

I see that Tony Grubb and Malcolm Gregson, products of Malvern and Millfield respectively and two of our more promising young professional golfers, are to spend the winter competing with the Arnold Palmers of this world on the tournament tour in the United States. Golf in America is altogether different from the game in this country: in some respects superior; in others, I think, otherwise.

Those of us who habitually go over there to write about major golfing events may perhaps have conveyed the false impression that every American club is a palatial affair, complete with swimming-pool and an entrance fee of £1,000. If so, we may be forgiven, for it is at this sort of club that these events are mainly played—which is one reason why I am for ever harping on the need to improve the public image of the clubs at which we entertain our visitors in return.

There are, in fact, some quite humble clubhouses among the smaller American clubs and, naturally enough among 5,500 of them, some very moderate courses, but, club for club, the amenities there are indeed palatial by comparison with here. A subscription of £150 a year, plus the compulsory spending of a minimum annual sum in the club—you never pay cash; you sign a chit, even for the caddie's tip—would, I think, be a fair average for a goodish country club, but this includes the whole family and they can all play and lunch and dine and dance and swim at the club, while Father is busy signing the chits.

Though Pine Valley, near Philadelphia, in my own opinion stands head and shoulders above any inland course in the world, there is a certain similarity in American courses—largely through accident of geography, I hasten to add—which undoubtedly gives us the edge in this respect. The vast majority are of what we should call the 'park' variety, though none the worse for that, reminiscent, of, say, Moor Park or Stoke Poges.

Grass in the States, despite the staggering advances made by 'agronomists', is still, on account of the climate, lush and coarse-bladed by comparison with ours at home—hence the American-sized ball. The little British ball tends to subside into the turf, and I am sure that quite a considerable number of points were lost through our team using it in the 1964 Ryder Cup match at Atlanta.

The main differences in golf in the two countries—and sometimes one thinks it really is a different game in America—may be summarized as 'slow play and stroke-play', the latter, incidentally, leading to the former. I will not elaborate on the all-too-familiar scene of slow play, except to say that one cause of it is the incessant picking-up and cleaning of balls on the green.

I mentioned some time ago having been told that professionals do this in order to replace the ball with the seam in line to the hole, believing that it will run more truly this way. A ballistics expert (or so I gather) writes to correct me. The facts, according to him, are as follows:

'Each ball has a bias or weighted side and will run accurately when this bias side is on top or bottom of the ball. If the bias is on the side of the ball, it will curve like a bowl (as used in bowls). The professionals use the main flash as a marker—not, as you state, with the seam in line to the hole but across the seam of the ball. In fact the ball has a long name flash which forms a distinct arrow on the ball when used for lining up the putt. This name flash is no accident but a carefully designed thing, so enabling the player to take advantage of this alignment aid.'*

As to stroke-play, from the very earliest days the Americans, logically enough, have looked upon golf as a business of going out and playing eighteen complete holes, certainly not picking your own ball up just because your four-ball partner has already won the hole. They want to see how many they can 'shoot'.

I possess somewhere, though I cannot for the life of me lay my hands on it, a copy of a letter written by the President of the USGA as long ago as 1901, urging American golfers in militant terms not to mind what the British did. So far as America was concerned, he declared, golf was and should continue to be a stroke-play game.

This topic also arose earlier this year when, making a night stop at the Mid-Ocean Club in Bermuda on the way back from Jamaica, I fell in with a party of four Roman Catholic priests on holiday from New York—the youngest having first approached me on the well-justified ground that I 'probably knew Dr Billy O'Sullivan, of Killarney'.

We all sat down for a 'jar' together, and they said that theirs was an annual outing, that they invariably played stroke-play and ended up by establishing one of their number as their 'champion'.

'After which,' I said, 'I suppose you light the scorecards and send up a column of white smoke!'

It took a moment or two for the penny to drop. When it did, their mirth was such that I feared it might do them permanent injury. If, as I suspect, this little story is gaining circulation in the State of New York—well, it was your correspondent who set it on its way.

* But see 'Maestro's Magnum Opus', p. 38.

MAESTRO'S MAGNUM OPUS

People sometimes ask me who is the best striker of a golf ball I ever saw and I reply without hesitation, 'Henry Cotton.' Nor does it yet seem likely that I shall have cause to revise this opinion. He seemed to reduce the frills of the golf swing to a minimum and simply to take the club in his immensely powerful hands in the most natural way and with them direct the ball to fly in a dead straight line towards the target—which it nearly always did.

I used to play with him a bit in his heyday, and one felt that, if all one had to do was that, then the game was comparatively simple after all—the result being that one's play improved immediately, if only temporarily, though I could always guarantee to hit one good drive by pretending that I was Cotton.* His own rifle-bullet straightness was proved at Muirfield in 1948 when he won his third Open championship fourteen years after his first, including five years 'off' for the war—and how is that for a method that 'repeats'? In four rounds he missed the fairway only four times in fifty-six drives.

Having thought so much about golf, and having come to certain firm conclusions about the golf swing which have stood the test of time, Cotton is now to my mind one of the great instructors in golf and, if I were an aspiring young professional, I would pay as much for one hour of his time—and probably get it for nothing—as for two of anyone else's.

The point of the above build-up is to say that he has now produced his magnum opus of golf instructions (*Study the Golf Game with Henry Cotton*, Country Life, 45s.), complete with no fewer than 750 photographs, and before I run out of superlatives I will say that it is not only the best illustrated but also the best documented that I have seen.

The book is also full of 'asides' which capture the interest. Talking, for instance, of some players' belief that you can see the line to the hole by dangling your putter vertically in line behind the ball and then looking at the shaft with your master eye (there can't be anything in this, surely, can there, though several famous people do it?), Cotton reveals that his own master eye is the left. There never was a better man than Cotton for 'hitting past the chin' and getting the ball on its way before letting his head move. Most of us are right-eyed. Being left-eyed, it occurs to me, gives the right-handed golfer an almost unfair advantage in keeping the head back!

Now that a single putt may mean a million dollars the portion of

* When I had used up this one, I would always guarantee one more by pretending I was Gene Sarazen.

the green immediately round the hole becomes more and more important. The experts peer into the hole, it seems, not to see if there is a frog in it but to see whether there is less soil showing above the metal rim on one side than the other. If so, they deduce that the ball will run in, if it is approaching the hole slowly, from the side on which the least soil is showing. We live and learn!

Cotton thinks that spikes on golf shoes are much too long and that the players who go out last are handicapped by all the marks around the hole. A player, he says, takes an average of 28 paces per green, which seems fair enough, and from this he produces the remarkable statistics that with 24 spikes this comes to 672 impressions per green or 12,096 per round. So on 18 greens 200 players leave 2,419,200 impressions in a single day.

Some time ago Cotton assured me that many professionals unnecessarily picked up and cleaned the ball so many times simply in order to replace it with the name pointing to the hole, since they believed it would run more truly this way. In 'Golf across the Water' I quoted an 'expert' correspondent who confirmed that there was indeed a bias on golf balls.

For myself I could not really believe this, and the theory has now been knocked on the head by a super-expert in the shape of the technical manager of a very well-known firm of manufacturers. 'If there was sufficient bias in a ball to affect a five-foot putt,' he says, 'what on earth do they think would happen to a 250-yard drive?' This seems completely convincing to me, but for good measure he adds that no ball can be more than $35/1,000$ of an inch out of centre without being automatically detected—and in any case, how could they guarantee that the bias, if any, would be in the same place in each ball?

Cotton in his book mentions that temperature affects the ball and that wise golfers in winter keep one ball in play and another warming up in the pocket. In the United States I have even seen advertisements for a 'pocket golf-ball warmer'. Was this, I asked the super-expert, an old wives' tale too? Rather to my surprise he said no, it wasn't. He himself, he added, always played two balls in winter.

The length of a golf ball depends on what they call the 'coefficent of restitution'—or the resuming of its original shape after compression on being struck. The late Lord Brabazon, incidently, was always seeking to reduce the length of the ball by setting a limit to this coefficient of restitution. At any rate, an impressive graph shows not only that a ball with the rubber frozen solid will hardly go at all, but, what is nearer home, that the difference between a ball at 32° Fahrenheit, the freezing-point of water, and at what we call 'normal' in our own body temperatures is no less than $19 \cdot 6$ yards in a carry of 240.

D

The curve rises almost imperceptibly after this and reaches its peak at 120°, after which it begins to go down through softening of the cover. Thus after all these years we learn at long last that the way to test the merits of a golf ball is not to tee it up and bash it but to take its temperature!

WITH THE EYES SHUT

I see that the Royal and Ancient Golf Club and the National Unions have combined in issuing a rather ponderous statement deploring the acceptance of gifts to celebrate doing a hole in one. I do not know what gifts one can wheedle out of people these days, but I should not have thought them sufficiently valuable to endanger one's amateur status, more especially as skill seems to play little or no part in deciding how often a man holes out in one.

Sandy Herd, it is true, did nineteen and James Braid eighteen. On the other hand Harry Vardon, one of the most accurate players of all time, did only one; Walter Hagen did only one and Walter J. Travis, the first overseas player to win the Amateur Championship, never did one at all.

Personally I have done two—the first many years ago when I was an undergraduate, the second only two or three years ago. On the second occasion it never occurred to me to ask anyone for anything— I thought that that sort of thing had all been forgotten—but on the first occasion I remember writing round to all sorts of people, which was the recognized thing in those days, and receiving not only the traditional bottle of whisky, some balls and a little stand on which to mount the ball, but also, believe it or not, an opera hat.

Today I suppose this would be severely frowned upon—especially the opera hat—but I must say that I looked on it in those days, as indeed I should today, as all good innocent fun and a kind of bonus for what is no more than a preposterous fluke, like drawing a straight flush at poker.

What does seem a little hard about holes in one is that the perpetrator is often expected to stand drinks to all present, caddies included, and his fluke may prove a very costly indiscretion. It set a friend of mine back no less than £17 the other day. A little later a man did the same hole in one but refused to entertain the company, on the ground that his ball had 'hit a tree first'. My own view is that the committee ought to give a standing order to the steward that any member doing a hole in one shall receive a bottle of whisky at the expense of the club.

How many people have done a hole in one? Some years ago the firm of Thresher and Glenny had the bright idea of designing a hole-in-one tie and were kind enough to ask my opinion as to whether there would be a sale for it. I consulted various friends and we tried to work out how many people per club had done a hole in one, and of these how many would bother to go and buy the tie.

As a result of profound calculations, and a lifelong knowledge of golf and golfers, I was able to proffer the expert opinion that there would be little future for such a tie. At the last count they had sold 45,000!

At this point permit me to introduce anyone who has done a hole in one to the Fanlingerers. When Hong Kong was overrun by the Japanese in 1941, Mr A. K. Mackenzie, the captain of the Royal Hong Kong Golf Club at Fan Ling, was totally blinded in the fighting. A past captain of the club, Mr Robert Young, escorted him home on the first ship to leave the colony after its liberation and saw him safely into the hands of the Scottish National Institution for War-Blinded.

Later on, Mr Young was the leading light in forming a society consisting of past and present members and friends of the Royal Hong Kong Club, with Mackenzie as the 'Taipan' or Number One. The Fanlingerers, of which I have the pleasure of being a member, meet twice a year, once in Scotland and once at the West Sussex Club at Pulborough, and their official objects are to enjoy each others' company and to aid the institution for war-blinded. There are now 890 members and they have raised the best part of £4,000.

Last year at Pulborough two members of the China Golfing Society who had won sixteen holes in a row in the afternoon match against Hong Kong asked one of their number, who is a jeweller, if he could devise something on which to mount the ball. From this arose a further request to mount a hole-in-one ball. The commission was carried out, and very attractive I can assure you it is.

No one, it was pointed out, would look at an order for less than 20,000, whereupon the inventor observed that, given the bits and pieces, he could put them together with his eyes shut. The penny dropped. This, after all, had originated at a meeting to aid the war-blinded. Why not hand it over to them? This was accordingly done, and now nearly every part is made and assembled by them.

What an admirable present for anyone who has done a hole in one—and never mind whether he still has the ball with which he did it. And how nice if clubs would keep some in stock to present with the compliments of the committee—instead of my suggested bottle of whisky!

I am hoping that this might become the standard mounting by which to celebrate holes in one. It will cost you 35s. from the Scottish Institution for War-Blinded, Linburn, Wilkieston, Midlothian, including about 10s. profit to the war-blinded and none to anyone else. And if you have not yet done a hole in one, well, keep a note of the address. It may be tomorrow.

SOME HAPPY HUNTING-GROUNDS

I am glad to see that my own part of the world is keeping up the time-honoured practice of freak golf matches. They not only keep the game from becoming too solemn but can also be extremely good fun. Last week, for instance, a combined team from Crowborough and Royal Ashdown Forest played a team of local archers, in three inches of snow, from the 10th tee at Ashdown to the last green at Crowborough, where the archers had to hole out by hitting a balloon.

It took them five and a half hours—the same time that it takes to play one round in the Canada Cup—and the archers won, as one imagines they almost must, by 84 to 102. They lost twelve arrows, which rather surprises me, and the golfers lost thirty-two balls, which doesn't.

For myself, I was inculcated into this particular form of golfing unorthodoxy in the celebrated after-tea one-club matches at Mildenhall, when we used to play a triangular course of three holes, sometimes as many as seven a side, from the 1st tee to the 2nd green, the 3rd tee to the 4th green and finally from the 5th tee over the fir trees to the 9th. The essence of such matches is, of course, that the players each carry a different club and must play strictly in rotation. A good deal of tactical thought thus comes into it, especially by the man with the putter, who can ruin the side's chances by putting the ball into spots where the man with the driver, who has to play next, can't play it.

When I touched on this subject once before, I found from correspondence that these long-hole matches were by no means unusual. I should like one day to play at the 'Northern Lake Rudolph Club', whose course consists, it appears, of two holes—the 'long first' which starts at the Abyssinian border and finishes twenty-seven miles later on at the Lokitaung river, and the 'short second', some eight miles along the gorge of the river, unplayable, it need hardly be said, in the rainy season. This latter was last played by a captain and lieutenant of the 4th King's African Rifles. It proved to be an immensely close match, the lieutenant winning by 3,923 shots to 3,950.

Only three years ago a rather splendid competition was played by eighteen bright young spirits at Hoylake. Attired in sweaters, gum-boots and bowler hats, they assembled at nine o'clock on a Sunday morning, each with one club of his own choosing and an unlimited supply of tennis balls, and set off to play, via the 17th hole, the road and the beach, a hole of about five and a half miles dead into a strong wind to the 18th at Heswell. The winner's score was 540, and one is not surprised to learn that at the end of it all 'most of the clubs were in a sorry state'.

Another capital hole, even nearer to my home on the top of the Downs, was invented for a foursomes match between a team consisting mainly of publishers and the TA Anti-Aircraft Regiment in Brighton. It stretched from Ditchling Beacon to the winning-post at Lewes Racecourse, where the trophy, a large Benares brass bowl, was sunk into the ground to serve as a hole. I am glad to record that my present publisher, Dr Desmond Flower, and his partner were the winners with a score of 113—and twenty-three lost balls.

In the match at Ashdown Forest the golfers took with them 100 balls, and, it is reported, would have lost the lot and run out of ammunition had it not been for the services of a white Alsatian called Penny, who spotted not only balls but arrows.

Though the retrieving of balls by dogs is comparatively common-place, it always intrigues me. It seems extraordinary that a golf ball can emit sufficient scent to betray its presence, even to the keenest-nosed dog. The delight in watching the dog work is of course by no means decreased by the satisfaction of getting something for nothing, more especially when it is clear that the previous owner can only have struck the ball two or three times before losing it.

At the Pyecombe club, a drive and a pitch, so to speak, from where I live, I remember watching the then professional training an exuberant spaniel puppy to retrieve balls and was surprised at how little time, no more than a fortnight, it took. At first the dog received a tiny piece of chocolate, thirty to the bar, each time, but now he will do it for nothing. The dog is still around the club, but there are only two members for whom he will retrieve. The others, if they rattle the chocolate tin, he will follow round but will not work for. With plenty of gorse bushes the club is a particularly happy hunting-ground and this dog, believe it or not, has found more than 4,000 balls in the past two years.

Huntercombe, where I spent many happy years, is another course with plenty of impenetrable gorse and thickets, and there used to be at least three dog-owners who divided the course up between them. I know of few more maddening experiences in golf than to see one of them waiting in exactly the right position for a high slice—and then to go and do it.

The dog at Pyecombe undoubtedly finds more balls when it is wet, so I suppose that it really is simply a matter of scent—and yet I wonder.

A long, long time ago I was out looking for balls with my old friend J. W. Moore, who retired last year after more than forty years' service with the Bedfordshire club, and at the fourteenth hole his dog started digging feverishly in the accumulated leaf-mould under the hedge. Having made a hole certainly eight inches deep, it then unearthed a ball—of a make that had not been manufactured for twenty years. Can this ball really have retained so penetrating a scent for so long—and, if not, how did the dog know it was there? We still await the expert answer. I had hoped to get it from a veterinary friend but all I could extract from him was that scent was 'a curious thing'. He produced a remarkable theory that it was liable to lie in layers since, when hunting, there were times when he, on his horse, could clearly scent a fox while hounds on the ground could not.

He also mentioned that dogs trained during the war had to detect, on their passing-out parade, mines that had been buried for three months. Someone suggested that they could scent the explosive. In fact there was none. They were dummies.

In support of the theory that there must be something more to it than merely scent, a Worthing correspondent quotes the case of his Jack Russell terrier which has been finding an average of eighteen balls per round for several years, with one record day of thirty-two. 'I cannot,' he says, 'throw any light on the question of how they do it but I can perhaps add to the confusion.'

This dog normally appears to detect by scent but there are some things which cannot be so explained. 'More than once I have seen him jump into a ditch containing a foot or so of dirty water and emerge immediately with a ball which, from the state of his nose, has clearly been dug out of the muddy bottom.

'Several times he has been seen to drop a ball which he has been bringing to me, dive several yards into thick bushes or gorse and to come out with another ball. Normally, of course, he would not drop a ball he was bringing in and yet in every case the position of the second ball has been such that it would seem impossible for him to have detected it by smell or sight from where the first ball was dropped.

'He has never been known to lift a ball in play—even though I have been playing a four-ball with strangers. He will help to search for a lost ball, uncover it, sniff it and leave it, although he is not nearly as good at finding such balls as one would expect. If during a search he finds a strange ball he will lift it immediately and he has even been known to lift a ball which is still being sought by other players, i.e., not playing with me.'

We may dismiss from the argument the Huntercombe member who many years ago used to carry his supply of balls in a bag impregnated with aniseed, but how can we account for the spaniel belonging to a lady in Haywards Heath which can not only detect balls in bushes or trees high above its head but, when out in the car, gets wildly excited when they so much as pass a golf course? It is a sobering thought that we golfers emit so powerful a scent as all that!

SLAMMING, WEDGING AND POPPING

One of the pastimes which must have been indulged in by golfers since the game began consists of picking a team—nowadays, I suppose, of fourteen—in which each man is assigned a club which he is to play throughout. In the United States the magazine *Golf Digest* picked three—for the driver, Sam Snead; for the wedge, Doug Ford; and for the putter, Bob Rosburg. They then produced books in collaboration with each of these three and these have now been published over here by Nicholas Kaye as a 'trilogy'.

The books are presented with admirable simplicity and, though they are strictly for the man who is prepared to use his intelligence in order to cut a few strokes off his game, there is much of human interest behind them.

Each incorporates an excellent idea which I have not seen since the days of Bobby Jones, when we used to have little 'flicker-books' of pictures—I still have mine—which, when flicked, showed the great man almost as though on a movie. These books have fifteen pages in the middle which, when flicked, do the same.

No one at any rate could cavil at the publisher's choice of model. 'Slamming' Sam Snead, as Byron Nelson says in a preface, did to the tee-shot in golf what Roger Bannister did to the four-minute mile. He showed that it was not good enough to hit it straight; to win, you had to hit it straight and far. Largely as a result, he enjoys what is perhaps the most remarkable record in the game's history.

In 1937 he won four tournaments and was runner up in the US Open; last year, twenty-seven years later, he still won an average of $2,000 in every tournament in which he played. When they started televising matches on a knock-out basis in 1958—at, I think $2,000 a time—Snead beat thirteen challengers in a row. Now, at fifty-two, he can still play thirty-six competitive holes—which means at least nine hours in America—in a day.

'Flicking' him over, I note that at the top of the swing Snead's left shoulder points not at the ball, but behind it. Having at the moment of writing been incarcerated for five days of my annual starvation cure and lost the equivalent of a full set of irons, including the putter, I find in the looking-glass that I can do this too. On the other hand I note also that, as Snead hits the ball and as his arms, straight as ramrods, pass through after it, his head is actually moving backwards. Try this one at your peril!

What is now known as the wedge was invented, in principle, by Sarazen in the early thirties and known then, and sometimes now, as a sand-iron. It is a club with a broad sole, the back edge of which is lower than the front, thus giving it 'bounce'—in other words you can hit down with it on sand or turf without its biting in and fluffing the shot. Probably the easiest club in the bag to play, and certainly the greatest reducer of scores, it is also the most neglected by the handicap golfer.

Doug Ford, born Fortunato, who plays so quickly as to have been described as 'the guy who looks as though he is playing through the group he is playing with', is the supreme master of the wedge. Under the intense pressure that only the finish of the Masters Tournament can arouse, he actually holed out from a bunker at the final hole to win. His explanations of how to play the ordinary 'splash' shot from sand, which looks so simple—and is—are as lucid as I have seen.

There are some who say that the wedge—together, of course, with raked bunkers—has so reduced the effect of these hazards that it ought to be banned. For myself I do not agree. I think the pleasure it could give to handicap players who are still afraid of sand (if only they knew about it) far outweighs the aggravation of having championship courses made to look silly by professionals.

The third author in the trilogy, Bob Rosburg, is a fellow after our own hearts. The son of a San Francisco doctor, he played for three years for Stanford University and did not turn professional until he was twenty-seven.

'I have a somewhat unorthodox swing,' he says, 'and people are always telling me I should change it. But whatever I've been doing wrong for thirty years I still do wrong. . . . I'm a slicer, so I just go ahead and slice and allow for it. That makes sense to me.'

Furthermore, he says he plays quite enough golf without wearing himself out in practising. 'I can't see practising—I may do a little putting, but that's about all.' About this, however, he makes two interesting points. He rarely practises putts of more than twelve feet; and he reckons to treat each practice putt as a separate entity, straightening himself up and re-gripping the club each time.

Rosburg, who once did a 62 with nineteen putts in eighteen holes—and next day took nineteen putts in the first nine—is the original 'pop' or, as some call it, 'tap' putter. He likes to give it a short, sharp blow rather than the smooth, flowing stroke on which most of us were brought up. The last thing he thinks of as he putts—and I confess it to be an entirely new one on me—is to make sure that the club is accelerating as it hits the ball.

'As long as the club-head is accelerating and makes a direct hit,' he says, 'I'm satisfied. With my pop stroke I don't care if I follow through or not, or even if the putter buries in the ground.' From which it seems that many of us have been 'popping', without knowing it, for a very long time—without, alas, the same results as Rosburg.

PARALYSIS BY ANALYSIS

Sixteen years ago when Ben Hogan, after being given up for dead by the roadside, recovered from the most frightful injuries to win both the US and British Open Championships, the Metropolitan golf writers of America hit on the idea of presenting a trophy to the golfer whom they thought had done most to overcome physical handicap and remain active in golf. Naturally the first recipient was Hogan himself, and thereafter it became an annual award. Last week they presented it to a seventy-seven-year-old expatriate Englishman, Ernest Jones.

Jones was born in Manchester and at the age of eighteen became assistant at Chislehurst, largely on account of his skill, even at that age, as a club-maker. He won the professional tournament known as the Kent Cup and then in 1915 went off to the war, where sixteen pieces of shrapnel cost him his right leg below the knee. Then, having won the Kent Cup on two feet before the war, he proceeded to win it again in 1920 on one.

Four years later the late Marion Hollins, a past US woman champion, invited him to go as professional to the new women-only club at Glen View on Long Island. People flocked to him for lessons, among them that greatest of all women golfers, Mrs 'Babe' Zaharias, who had become in her own phrase 'fouled up in the mechanics of the game', and later, when the club was taken over by men, he established himself on the seventh floor of a building on Fifth Avenue and became undoubtedly the most popular indoor teacher in the history of golf.

Jones's phenomenal success with his pupils, at least one of whom came to regard his teaching almost as a religion, was due, I think, to its simplicity. 'Swing the club-head,' was his maxim. Or, again, 'You cannot move the club faster than you can swing it.' As evidence of this, he would tie a jack-knife to his handkerchief and swing this and the club together. A good smooth swing brought the two 'club-heads' to the ball at the same moment. Any form of jerk left the jack-knife behind.

There is no doubt that the ball can be hit both well and far with a solid head on the end of a flexible shaft. That supreme trick-shot artist Paul Hahn—whose show should on no account be missed if he comes over here again—demonstrates with a block of wood on the end of a piece of garden hose. I tried it myself and can confirm that all you have to do, as Jones insists, is to 'swing the club-head'.

Nevertheless, on the basis that a cat may look at a king, and admitting that my knowledge of physics is nil, I believe that it is his simplicity, rather than his mechanics, that has made Jones such a successful teacher. 'Those who think in terms of golf being a science,' he says, 'have unfortunately tried to part from each other the arms, head, shoulders, body, hips and legs. They turn the golfer into a worm cut into bits, with each part wriggling in every-which-way direction.' He calls it 'paralysis by analysis'.

Here I feel he is undoubtedly right. If we had an analysis, plus anatomical diagrams, of the muscles and movements involved in getting a fork into one's mouth—where one can't even see the 'ball', let alone keep one's eye on it—most of us would either stab ourselves or starve.

On the other hand would the physicists agree with the following? 'The greatest force you can develop with a given amount of power is centrifugal in nature. It is achieved by swinging. It is not necessary to quote from the science of physics for proof. Even ancient man understood that a swinging action developed maximum force. Remember David and Goliath and think: how did David get the force into the stone?'

It may be assumed that David, using rather a flat swing, slung the stone. He did, as the headhunting Dyak in Borneo observed to the missionary who showed him a picture of the incident in an illustrated edition of the Old Testament, 'secure a particularly fine head'— and presumably by centrifugal force. One cannot help asking, however, whether he would not have done even better with the aid of some powerful catapult elastic.

Jones also cites the case of the pendulum, which, however long or short its backswing may be, applies its maximum force at the bottom of the swing, simply by swinging. This, again, is presumably true— but what about if Arnold Palmer caught hold of it half-way down its swing and gave it the old one-two? A photograph would show the shaft of the pendulum, if it did not snap in half, bent backwards like a bow. Surely, if Jones is right, the makers of golf shafts have been wasting their time since the game began. Surely with a steel shaft, as against a handkerchief or a piece of hosepipe, Palmer can move the club faster than he can swing it.

Again, Jones says categorically, 'There is only one swing: the correct one.' Well now, once more I take leave to wonder. I repeat the words of the 1964 Open Champion, Tony Lema—leaving blanks since you may derive some innocent amusement in trying to detect the players before looking at the answers:

If you examine the swings that many of the successful players use, you might well decide that not one of them is any good.
(1)——lunges at the ball and punches it.

(2)——has the unorthodox habit of letting his right elbow ride far out from his body as he takes the club back.

(3)——has such a loop at the top of his backswing that it makes him look as though he were waving a flag. I myself loop noticeably at the top.

(4)——is all hands and wrists like a man dusting the furniture.

(5)——has his wrists almost completely cocked before he has even started his swing.

(6)——braces himself with a wide stance that looks like a sailor leaning into a north-east gale and takes the club back barely far enough to get it off the ground.

If you lined all these players up on the practice tee without knowing who in the world they were and asked them to hit a few shots your advice would be simple: 'Go back and sell insurance. You haven't got it.'*

None of which alters the fact that Ernest Jones is a very great teacher and thoroughly deserves his award.

* The answers are: (1) Arnold Palmer; (2) Jack Nicklaus; (3) Jacky Cupitt; (4) Julius Boros; (5) Jerry Barber; (6) Doug Sanders.

DIABOLICAL ANTICS

Six years ago it came to my knowledge that that great and, some would say, eccentric practitioner in the art of golf-course architecture, Tom Simpson, had expressed a wish that he could see the obituary I should write of him. I therefore with his co-operation did it in advance in these columns and, much delighted, he sent copies to all his friends. It was not until last year that, at the age of eighty-seven, he died.

Now for these past few days it has been for me as though he were living again, for by a coincidence I have had in my hands, and only wish that I could keep, two extraordinary books which recall his life and thoughts and work. The first, handsomely bound in leather and surely unique, is entitled in gold letters *Golf Architect's Bible*, but far from being the printed treatise one might expect, is in fact a lifetime compilation of notes, writings and cuttings by Simpson himself, ranging from A for 'Ants and Cockchafers' to W for 'Worms'. It is now the property of his fellow architect Mr C. K. Cotton.

The contents of Tom's 'bibles' are far from so prosaic as Ants and Worms. In the flyleaf, starting as he means to go on, the compiler has written in bold red ink: *Ninety per cent of the criticisms made by club members are due to Invincible Ignorance.* Also on the flyleaf are, unaccountably, the initials CVLH, which can only indicate Mr C. V. L. Hooman, who played in the first two Walker Cup matches in 1922 and 1923. Tom not only wrote out and assembled almost everything that a golf architect could need to know but added many of the touches that made him such a 'character'. Here, for instance, is a list of 'things to take on visits'—all eighty of them, including not only passport, protractors, plans, etcetera, but, less obviously, bananas, bible and seasickness remedy!

Here, too, is pasted a list of 'stock phrases' for use with—or perhaps I should say against, for he fought a running battle with them all his life—club committees.

The club having been informed that their course is 'far from attractive' the stock phrase runs 'we would stress the importance of beauty in all construction work. Beauty is difficult to define, as is the taste of sugar, but is none the less very real. Those who appreciate it take off their shoes. The rest just sit around and eat blackberries.'

Another 'stock phrase', emphasizing the subtle quality of the Old Course at St Andrews, seemed to strike a chord. And guess who wrote it. Yes, honestly! Thirty years ago. Another stock phrase reminds clients that humdrum holes are no good and that 'it is only the mad masterpieces that remain in the memory'. Among them are included the 12th, 13th, 14th, 16th and 17th at St Andrews, the 4th and 17th at Woking, the 14th at Liphook, and the 13th at West Sussex.

Tom Simpson was a great keeper of personal books. He had a magnificent 'Wine Book', which he had compiled from his own vast experience and which he once lent me, and a big cuttings book of miscellaneous items written by or about him. This he left to Dr S. Pope, a past captain of Liphook, and I have it before me now.

Simpson himself lived at Liphook and always claimed, as so many do today, that it combined skill and pleasure in ideal proportions. It has only fifty bunkers, against an average of a hundred and twenty; you can get round comfortably twice in a day, and in forty-two years no one, including Bobby Locke, has done better than 69. His relations with the club he loved so well were not, however, uniformly harmonious. When he suspected that the committee were meeting to demand his resignation, so Dr Pope tells me, he caused himself to be driven slowly up and down in his Rolls-Royce in front of their window.

Simpson was all against length for length's sake and all in favour of luck. He liked his courses to demand 'mental agility'. Golf, he thought, should be 'a game of real adventure as against an examination of stroke production . . . . should combine a pleasant form of physical vigour with the problems of the chessboard'. Or again, 'No tee shot can possibly be described as good if the proper place to be is the centre of the fairway. . . .' 'The vital thing about a hole is that it should either be more difficult than it looks or look more difficult than it is. It must never be what it looks.'

This attitude, when translated on the ground, led him into much trouble, and I have been re-living the controversies that arose from his work at Rye and on the New Course at Sunningdale. Golfers in their 'invincible ignorance' did not like being teased by what Bernard Darwin called his 'diabolical antics', and in fact both these works were later changed.

He also, from his worship of St Andrews, where on at least six holes no part of the green is visible, was a great believer in showing only half the flagstick and this failed to find favour too. A case in point was his short 14th at Rye. I do not think that any who can remember this semi-blind hole will compare it favourably with the late Sir Guy Campbell's brilliant replacement.

Nevertheless, his meticulous plans, estimates and accounts show what a competent man of business he was, for all his occasional quirks and fancies on the course. The closeness of his estimates to actual cost is astonishing, and the planemakers of today will be shaken to know that on occasions the former actually exceeded the latter.

At Rye, for instance, he estimated £1,460 and the cost was £1,374. 6s. 6d. (the 14th green and tee, complete, cost £250 in 1932. I suppose it would be £1,000 today). At Sunningdale, he estimated £7,912 against £7,748. 16s. 3d.; Muirfield, £473 against £443. 2s. 8d.; Ashridge, £2,461 against £2,587. 16s. 6d.; Woking (25 men at 1s. an hour) £409 against £423. 11s. 9d.

How many people, I wonder, have private courses today? In Tom Simpson's pre-war brochure for prospective clients he quotes having built private courses for Lord Louis Mountbatten, Sir Phillip Sassoon, Bt, Sir Archie Birkmyre, Bt, Sir Mortimer Singer, Bt, and a commoner by the name of Mr James de Rothschild. The pictures and description of the exquisite—and diabolical—little pitching-and-putting course (estimate £685, cost £665) which he built for the then owner, Mr William Clark, in the gardens of Windlesham Moor, fascinates me too. Is it there, I wonder, today? And, if so, can anybody hole it, as Joyce Wethered did on the opening day, in 28?

'A GOOD GAME FOR CONVERSATION'

I should not have ventured to refer in this column to the giant whose passing we have been mourning—or in my own case, as with many others, applauding, for we feel more like members who stand and clap as the century-maker returns to the pavilion at the conclusion of a great innings—had it not been for the extraordinary coincidence of coming across a reference to him in, of all things, a life of James Braid by Bernard Darwin.

I knew that Sir Winston in his day had 'had a go' at golf, as indeed most things, but gathered that the game had not greatly appealed to him. I have before me a picture of him in action, attired in a somewhat cramping blue serge suit, grey homburg hat, and shoes which appear to be devoid of either rubber or nails, and it is clear that he has taken a characteristically vigorous swipe at the ball.

He is back on the right foot, his left toe is in the air and from the position of the hands and arms one may deduce that his style, like that of so many of us, tended to be 'over and round' rather than, as the professionals exhort, 'under and through'. I should be surprised if informed that this particular shot achieved any great degree of loft.

Like other contemporary statesmen—Lloyd George, Masterman and, keenest of them all, Arthur Balfour—Sir Winston used frequently to repair to Walton Heath, where James Braid reigned as professional for nearly fifty years. 'Mr Churchill,' wrote Darwin, 'was never a distinguished exponent of the game, but in those days it was almost necessary, if you wanted to be in touch with the latest political movement, to play golf at Walton Heath, and by selecting Braid as his partner Mr Churchill was able to get the maximum exercise and win a fair proportion of matches, while not unduly hampering the efforts of the other players.'

What really does astonish me is that Braid, the wisest of men, always regarded Sir Winston as the authentic inventor of that form of golf known as the 'greensome'—in which, for the uninitiated, both partners drive at each hole and then, having selected the more propitious of the two drives, continue with alternate shots as a foursome. I find this difficult to believe, but one can hardly declare that Sir Winston did not invent it unless one can say who did, and this I certainly cannot do. Can anyone, I wonder?*

How much one would give to have been present at some of these

* Undoubtedly, it would now seem, Sir Lycett Green, of Norfolk.

'political' games at Walton Heath! Sir Winston, it appears, declared that golf was a 'good game for conversation'. Lloyd George, a keener though I doubt whether a more effective performer, who played at St Germain during the Peace Conference in Paris after the First World War, said to a friend, 'Golf is much the best game. It takes place in the open air, you play with beauty all round you, you get exercise and you can talk all the time.'

Another of the Walton Heath coterie was the presiding genius of the club, who later became Lord Riddell. Of him Darwin wrote: 'He was a remarkable golfer in that he was inclined to talk continuously on all sorts of subjects during the round and yet keep his mind on the match, which he very properly liked to win.'

Braid himself was the most silent of men, as well as the most discreet. Many of the deepest political secrets of the day must have come his way in those weekly games at Walton, but to the end of his life, even when it could no longer matter, he gave none away.

Though I am old enough to have played with him on one or two occasions, I knew him only when he had already become almost a Mr Chips of golf. As the talk flowed in the clubhouse after the game, he would survey the company with an occasional twinkle in his eye and the tolerant indulgence of one who had heard it all, and seen it all, before.

Few of the great players have possessed the temperament to enjoy golf as a 'good game for conversation'. A substantial number manage to acquire all the shots: the champions come from among the few who attain also the ability to weave a sort of cocoon of concentration round themselves, so that they can produce the shot when it matters most.

The nearest approach to a conversational champion was, I suppose, Walter Hagen, who was always ready with a greeting or a 'crack' for the faithful who followed him round. He developed the knack of switching his mind off and on, so to speak, as he walked round, and on arriving within thirty yards of his ball would fade away and within a few seconds be again wrapped completely in the business of winning the championship. Yet even he, I am assured, was so unnerved by the sudden apparition of the Prince of Wales to watch him at Sandwich that he hit his next shot hard on the head.

Hagen's apparent lightheartedness was in itself an insurance against being thrown out of gear by the type of idiot who at the critical moment in the championship would come up and say, 'You don't remember me. I met you when you played in that exhibition match at Little Puddlescombe. . . .'

Nowadays the champions play in silent splendour in a roped-off

E

arena, and we are permitted neither to address nor to listen to them, nor even indeed to take pictures of them. Perhaps they still converse as they go grimly round in pursuit of their enviable millions. One thing, however, is certain. Their conversation is not as entertaining as Sir Winston's must have been.

SLUGGERS AND SWINGERS

In a field composed otherwise of professionals, assistants, and first-class amateurs, it was good to see two women players surviving to the last day of the Sunningdale Foursomes and one of them, Mrs Spearman, with her large and cheerful professional partner, Tony Fisher, winning it. The other, Mrs Anderson, who used to be Jean Donald, has the distinction, if such it may be considered, of being one of the two women players who have beaten me level—a fate more pleasant perhaps than death but one to which I have taken care never to expose myself again.

Considering its beginnings compared with that of men, the rise in ability in women's golf has been extraordinary. In an age when it was held indecorous to raise the club above the shoulder and the clothing virtually prevented their doing so in any case, women golfers were confined to little pitching and putting courses of their own. The men had been holding an amateur championship for the best part of twenty years before the ladies progressed as far as forming their Golf Union.

The meeting which did so in 1893 was attended by representatives of eleven clubs, and I wonder how many people could guess the names of them today? They were, as a matter of interest: Great Harrowden Hill, St Andrews, Barnes, Eastbourne, Blackheath, Southdown and Brighton, Holywood, Minchinhampton, Ashdown Forest, Wimbledon and Lytham St Annes.

The Chair was taken at this meeting by that great Scottish golfer, then settled in Wimbledon, Dr Laidlaw Purves, the man who discovered Sandwich Bay as a golfer's paradise and became the first captain of Royal St George's.

He harangued the ladies present on the desirability of working out a uniform code of rules and a system of handicapping. 'It is a calumny,' he said, 'to suggest that woman is incapable of a mature and seasoned interest in golf.

'If you can persuade clubs to revert to the old Scottish game, as it existed before the innovations introduced by St Andrews during the last twenty years, you will have achieved a large amount of success.' These are stern words. To what I wonder, was he referring—and are these wicked innovations with us still today?

The Ladies Golf Union which was formed that day certainly got down to the business of handicaps, and I am amazed at the regimentation up with which they put for their own good today. Despite pleas that many women cannot, and never will, play to a handicap of 36—some indeed never having broken 130—36 remains the limit.

In the old days the limit was apparently 50 and even this, it is clear, was not enough. I have before me the results of a competition played at Bowdon, Cheshire, in the nineties. Of the ten players, four had a handicap of 50 and two were 40. The winner was Mrs Dallmyer with the clearly remarkable score of 89-8-81. The next best player, handicap 20, had 132-20-112, and trailing at the end was poor little Miss Pocock (one feels she must have been little) with 254-50-204. It was Mrs Dallmyer, incidentally, who committed, I need hardly say inadvertently, one of the cruellest acts ever recorded in golf. Playing top for Ganton against another Yorkshire club, she won all the first nine holes—and then did the 10th in one!

It seems astonishing that only twenty years or so should have separated the pat-ball age of women's golf and the emergence first of Miss Cecil Leitch and then after the war interval of Miss Joyce Wethered, of whom it has been said by knowledgeable critics that, if women could have played in the Walker Cup match, she should have been no lower than number four.

I think it was when she had given up amateur competitive golf that she played with Charles Yates, later to become British Amateur Champion in 1938, against Miss Dorothy Kirby and Bobby Jones at East Lake, Atlanta. This was the home course of the three Americans. Miss Wethered was seeing it for the first time.

'In sheer power,' recorded Grantland Rice, 'Miss Wethered's game was bewildering.' At the 17th, when Yates confessed that he had never hit a better drive in his life and his ball caught the down-slope for added length, Miss Wethered's was found to be no more than a dozen yards behind. 'I don't believe it,' said Yates. 'No woman can hit the ball that far.' In the end Jones beat her only by 2 and 1 and she beat Yates by one hole. As I found at the 1963 Ryder Cup match, this game is still talked about at East Lake.

Yet when Joyce played the next great phenomenon in women's golf—to say nothing of Olympic athletics—the late Mrs Babe Zaharias, the latter was far from impressed. 'It was not too unusual,' she wrote in her remarkable book *This Life I've Led*, 'for me to get tee-shots of 280-300 yards or more. The other women did not slug the ball that way. Take Joyce Wethered, the British star. She was one of the women golfers I used to read about when I was a kid growing up. I got to play against her a couple of times. She had a beautiful swing. She'd been classed by quite a few experts as the finest swinger in the game, man or woman. And that was the way of golf over in England or Scotland. You didn't hit the ball. You swung at it. The idea was to develop a nice graceful swing.

'But Joyce Wethered didn't hit the ball very far. I think I could have taken a two-iron and driven it past where she hit her wood. I don't mean that she wasn't a great all-round player. She and I scored about the same in our two matches. But in women's golf today you've got to have that distance. You've got to be a slugger as well as a swinger.'

It is a relief to think that, whether they slug it or swing at it, I need never find myself playing any of them level again.

'Then and Now' is a topic that has always fascinated me. Golf has changed more completely than games like football and cricket and baseball; not only the ball, the implements, and the condition of the courses, but also the clothing—and especially the clothing of the women.

How much it has changed has been brought home to me on studying with great delight a book called *Ladies' Golf*, written by Miss May Hezlet, champion in 1899 and 1902, and published in 1904. This was picked up for 6*d*. by a friend in St Ives, who very kindly sent it to me on the charitable and accurate assumption that I was 'often looking for something to write about'. The author herself appears on the frontispiece in what is obviously her Sunday best—a big flat fur hat, fur collar and neat fur muff. On a pedestal beside her sits her smooth-haired fox terrier, his head knowingly on one side in the familiar 'His Master's Voice' pose. A pretty, wide-eyed girl.

I cannot truthfully say how well they played in those days but however well they did, they did it in spite of their clothes. Anything more calculated to impede the golf swing it would be difficult to design. Not that one would call their clothes downright unattractive, like, for instance, those of the 'Boy Friend' period: they seem to me to be 'negative'—which perhaps, when you come to think of it, is what they were meant to be. The female form was doubtless divine but the golf course was no place in which to demonstrate the fact. Nor, however fine a head of hair you had, would you think of taking to the links without a whacking great hat or bonnet.

Blouse, or tie and blouse, and coat covered the top half, while the 'limbs', as I believe they were called, were totally obscured by a voluminous skirt which left all to the imagination except a glimpse of buttoned boot which peeped coyly forth in the course of the swing. I had hoped to see a picture of a 'Miss Higgins' in action, but perhaps it is the wrong period or the champions dispensed with this artificial aid. A 'Miss Higgins', so named after its inventor, was an elastic band which was in some way hitched round the skirt half-way down, in order to keep it out of the way.

The girls of yesteryear may have been impeded by their clothes, but, my word, how they did bash away at the ball, and what beautiful swings some of them had! Here, I see for instance, is Miss Lottie Dod, semi-finalist in 1898 and 1899, driving at what I take to be one of the sleeper-bunkered holes at Westward Ho! She looks charming in her broad-brimmed straw boater, white blouse and tie and big white skirt, but the point is that if by a trick of photography you could clothe her in modern attire she would do admirably as an illustration for *How to play Golf in the Sixties*.

I am glad to see, too, a couple of pictures of Miss Rhona Adair, who, like Miss Hezlet, hailed from Ireland and won the championship in 1900 and 1903.

Miss Adair has been my pin-up girl of golf ever since I first saw her in the gallery of mounted cut-out pictures which are such a feature of the Lady Golfers' Club in Whitehall and in which her finish is almost indistinguishable from that of Ben Hogan. In one of the pictures now before me, taken from directly behind, she is again at the finish of a drive and clearly, as P. G. Wodehouse put it, 'has not spared herself in her effort to do the ball a violent injury'. Her left elbow as we look at her from behind is stretched horizontally out behind her, and the head of the club is almost horizontally out in front. Let middle-aged readers try that one and see!

As to the clothes of today, let every man judge for himself. For myself I would have settled for the style of about fifteen to twenty years ago, when women golfers had become emancipated so far as clothing is concerned but were still essentially feminine in appearance. Trousers on some of the girls look enchanting, but not, heaven help us, on all. For myself, I am an anti-shorts man, certainly at any rate in this country, where it is never really warm enough to warrant them. Bermuda shorts are, it is true, the most modest of garments. I trust that that is not why I do not like them—but I don't. I find them ghastly on either sex.

AS RENDERED BY NICKLAUS

Those who aspire to golfing fame and fortune in the United States must be prepared among other things, according to an analysis made during the last two Open Championships, to drive a ball consistently 250–70 yards, onto a fairway less than 35 yards wide; hit the long iron more than 200 yards and within 36 feet of the flag; hit the medium iron 150–75 yards and within 26 feet, i.e. 6 per cent of the original distance; and putt within 4 feet from 75 feet, 2·4 from 40, and 1·8 from 30. Furthermore, 'under all conditions and on every variety of green', they must hole all putts up to 2 feet, half of all the 6-footers and one in ten of the 25-footers.

This might well be a definition of Jack Nicklaus—despite Sam Snead's declaring at a recent dinner in New York that he is now, at the age of twenty-five years and a few days, as good as he ever will be and faces only the problem of how long he can stay on top. The evergreen Snead himself remains one of the world's finest golfers and can still pick a ball out of the bottom of the hole without bending his knees—and how many of our readers, I wonder, can do that at the age of fifty-three. 'These kids,' he says, 'are like high-strung thoroughbred horses. They're nothing but a bunch of nerves, and you can't take that very long.' Bobby Jones, he recalled, retired at twenty-eight.

Warming to his theme, Snead added that both he and Ben Hogan would still be contenders for major championships if it were not for their putting. 'We can still get from tee to green as well as most of them but it's getting the ball in the hole that kills us. Once you get the yips there's nothing you can do about them. Once you got 'em, you keep 'em for ever.'

We have among us, however, a shining example to prove that this is not wholly true. Mr Alec Hill, captain of the Royal and Ancient Golf Club of St Andrews, was for many years afflicted with this complaint, which, ludicrous though it may sound to the outsider, has caused many a sane and sober man to give up golf altogether. The rest of us simply take to putting croquet-fashion between our legs— and the first professional to realize how deadly this can be will, I prophesy, sweep the board and thus probably result in the croquet-putter being banned.*

I do not profess to know what goes on in Mr Hill's mind these days and, as a fellow sufferer, would certainly not bring up the evil topic in conversation, but the fact is that, having driven himself in

* A forecast which in 1967, alas, proved only too true.

as captain, he went on to win the Medal and you can hardly do that
and be a prey to the 'yips' at the same time. If he could reveal to the
world how he overcame them, his year of captaincy would be
memorable indeed.

With regard to the great Hogan, who strikes the ball as well as ever
but now gets 'stuck' on the green, unable to move his hands or the
club or anything, I have a certain twinge of conscience, because during
the course of the 1958 Canada Cup in Mexico City I told him, little
thinking, my story of the Austrian doctor.

Some years ago when I had been writing about the 'twitch', as it is
more commonly known in this country, the doctor wrote to say
that he specialized in this sort of thing and that if I came to see him
he would gladly reveal the secret. I repaired post-haste to Harley
Street and he alleged that the whole ghastly disease sprang from the
angle of the right elbow. He then added, almost casually, 'As a matter
of fact violinists get it.'

What a truly appalling thought! One imagines the hushed Albert
Hall, the solitary figure spotlighted on the stage. He manages the bits
with the right arm outstretched and the twiddly bits under the chin,
but half-way across, with the elbow bent as in putting, there is suddenly
a convulsive twitch and he has nearly sawn the thing in half. From
that moment he knows he will never play in public again.

This was the tale which with suitable gestures I told Hogan as we
sat on the terrace at Mexico City—forgetting that in an effort to win
his fifth Open Championship he had, when faced with a three-foot
putt on the 71st, 'sawn it in half'. A glazed look came over his eye,
but it was too late now. From that period Hogan was never quite the
same and I sometimes wonder guiltily whether I contributed to this
fact. How tactless can you be?

Nicklaus has had his bad spells on the green but does not yet, I
fancy, know what it is to look at a yard putt and see it suddenly take
on the aspect of a particularly deadly and poisonous snake. He does,
however, know that it is possible to miss them, and I pass on a tip
in this connection from his latest book *My 55 Ways to Lower Your
Golf Score*. Having written the above I turned to the piece in question,
and from the last two lines it is clear that his experience, or at least
his imagination, is rather greater than one had suspected.

'My practice as an amateur,' he says—and I suppose he never plays
match-play now, poor fellow—'was always to make my opponent
putt the short ones on the first couple of holes, concede them in the
middle of the match, and then, when the match was tight in the
closing holes, make him putt them again. The reason for this is simple.
On the first two or three holes the short putts are harder because

nobody has settled down. In the closing holes of a tight match they can be harder still if you haven't had to try putting for a dozen or so holes. The hole is suddenly going to look as small as a thimble and your putter will feel about as secure in your hands as a live snake.'

I sometimes wonder whether the likes of me—I will not say 'us'—can really be helped by the likes of Nicklaus. He cannot have any conception, fortunately enough, of what it feels like to be me. Tuck a pillow in the front of his trousers, enfeeble his left eye, drain three-quarters of the strength from his hands and fingers, make him pant when walking up slopes and cause the blood to rush to his head if the ball falls off the tee and he has to bend down to pick it up again, and he might begin to get the idea.

On the other hand it is nice for the likes of us to imagine what it must be like to feel like Nicklaus, who glories in his strength and cheerfully invites the young to do the same. My own generation was always taught to try and cultivate a good swing and let distance come later. Nicklaus thinks exactly the opposite.

'The first thing I learned was to swing hard, and never mind where the ball went. That is the way Arnold Palmer was taught, too, and I think it is the right way. A youngster first trying golf will enjoy the game more if allowed to whale away at the ball, and he will be developing the muscles he needs to become a strong hitter. Once he has achieved distance, he can learn control while still hitting a long ball.'

The most important factor in long hitting, he thinks—and it would be interesting to know how many long hitters feel the same—is strength in one's legs, and this is developed by hitting hard when one is young. 'If a golfer does this while young, he will get the leg strength needed to hit very long shots. I know that my distance is due more to the strength in my legs than to any power I might be getting from my arms, hands, or fingers.'

Meanwhile, spring draws us from our winter lairs and a few tentative swings may soon be made with the special weighted club, if we can find it. '250–70 yards to a fairway 35 yards wide; long irons over 200 yards to within 36 feet. . . .' I can see them all! As rendered by Nicklaus.

'AS GOOD AS YOU HAVE TO BE'

The United States Golf Association, having calculated that in the four main stroke-play events of 1964 the average winning score was 276, whereas twenty-five years ago it was 284·3, or just over two strokes per round higher, asked a number of professionals past and present, together with golf architects and writers, why this should be. Courses are habitually made tougher and tighter for these events. Clubs and balls have scarcely changed. How comes it that the winning standard has so noticeably improved?

Some say it lies in the putting. Byron Nelson, for instance, who had the misfortune to become one of the six greatest players in the game's history just at the wrong time, namely during the war years, says, 'In my day there were a few good putters. Today everyone is a good putter.' Charles Bartlett of the *Chicago Tribune* says, 'I am not going to budge from my stand that the name of the game is putting!'

Tommy Armour always maintained that the rapid improvement in scoring came almost wholly from the invention of the wedge, which in the hands of a player of only modest competence takes away all the terrors of bunker play. This view is shared by our own Leonard Crawley, who in addition cites 'American watered greens of superb texture'.

Jim Barnes, the tall Cornishman who emigrated to America and won their Open Championship in 1921 and ours in 1925, says bluntly, 'Today's fairways are better than a lot of the greens we played on. Most of the rough they land in today you can hit a 4-wood out of and hold the shot on the green. If you hit a 4-wood to the kind of greens we had, you would never find the ball again.'

I am sure it is true to say that in America—I do not know that it would apply here—the surface condition of courses has vastly improved, even in the past twenty-five years.

The Americans have more difficult problems of climate, some of the courses in the North being closed and under snow for much of the winter, others in the South only playable when it is cool enough for the grass to grow. At the Augusta National, for instance, all the fairways are ripped up in mid-April after the Masters, the course closed, and everything resown for the autumn. These climatic problems are now being spectacularly overcome by the 'agronomists' with their new strains of grass.

The main reason given for improved scoring is, however, one which I myself am convinced to be principally the answer. It is put succinctly by that great diminutive player, Paul Runyan, who in his prime would surely have been murdered by the mighty bashers of today—and the more's the pity. 'A champion,' he says, 'is as good as he has to be.'

Jack Nicklaus, whose recent 271 in the Masters will help to keep this year's average down, thought that last year's low scoring was 'basically the result of very favourable weather conditions', but added, 'I also believe that the fellows just had to play better because the competition is keener.' Ken Venturi, who made such a heart-warming comeback from three barren years to win the US Open—only to have his game set back again, possibly for ever, by some kind of trouble in his hands—says simply, 'We have more good scores today because we have more good players.' Tony Lema, British Open Champion in 1964, says, 'The number of good players increases every year, and so does the number capable of winning a major tournament.'

All the same, it probably boils down to being 'as good as you have to be'. If you no longer get your name in the papers by running a mile in four minutes, you run it in less. If 284 is no good and a million dollars is waiting for 276, then somehow or other they will average 276. I wonder, nevertheless, whether there is something in a point which none of the experts mentions, namely that man himself is increasing in size and strength?

In Japan, so they say, a suit which fitted a man before the war now only fits a boy. Whether this is true I cannot swear but as a very broad generalization I believe it is true in the United States, at any rate among professional golfers. At the last hole at Augusta—420 yards and all uphill—Nicklaus was reaching the green with a drive (about 350 yards) and a wedge. One day he reached the second, 555 yards with the second shot downhill, with a drive and a 5-iron.

There have always been the mighty hitters of their day but in the old days they were 'seen off' by the supremely skilful. James Braid was tall and lanky and probably the longest hitter of the 'Great Triumvirate', but Harry Vardon and J. H. Taylor were of modest dimensions. Could they, I wonder, given equal equipment, conditions and age, i.e. twenty-five, have stood up, for all their skill, to anyone with the bull-like strength of Nicklaus and the ability to hit the ball straight?

Could Jones, who was always reckoned to have twenty yards in hand from the tee, to be unloosed only when required, have stood up to being outdriven by perhaps sixty yards? Could Hagen or Sarazen? The golfing skill and technique needed by Jones in 1927 to hole the Old Course at St Andrews in 68 with hickory shafts and to win the Open with 285 were almost certainly greater than those possessed by Nicklaus today, but could they have prevailed, given like conditions, against this modern howitzer?

Arnold Palmer has recently revealed his conception of the perfect golf course, ideal as a test of skill and enjoyment both for the club member and the giant such as himself. It is significant that this course, 'primarily because golfers today learn to hit hard and long before they learn any other aspect of the game', measures 7,080 yards. The four par-5 holes measure 490, 525, 570, and 620 yards—and even then, he reckons, some of the howitzers will take a chance on reaching the closely guarded greens in two!

The thought of spending five hours plodding round a course of 7,080 yards casts a melancholy on my soul. Nevertheless, it is equally wretched that the finest players of their generation should find no course in the world capable of demanding the full range of their talent and be reduced to walking 555 yards for the pleasure of hitting a drive and a 5-iron.

The solution, of course, is so blindingly simple that one would not expect anyone to give it a passing thought. There should be a special and shorter 'tournament ball' for 'them' and another, the present one, for 'us'. Then all could play happily together on the same course at the same time—and might even do it, as their fathers did, twice in one day.

STONE THE CROWS!

It would seem that, despite the efforts of well-meaning gentlemen to adjust the standard scratch scores of golf courses and in the process cause our handicaps to bear some nearer relation to our capabilities, the intended improvement has not yet found its way to the Home of Golf, St Andrews. At the Spring Meeting of the Royal and Ancient Club last week I was interested, as always, to note how the net scores—every one of which theoretically ought to be in the neighbourhood of 73—compared with this target.

I hope I shall not be accused of commenting on the domestic affairs of the club if I say that the handicapping committee are a pretty hard-hearted body of men, ever willing to suspect the worst and to keep a man at a handicap of, say, one for at least ten years before finally raising him to two at a time of life when he can no longer play to eight. Even so, it would seem that the members of the R. and A., some 230 of whom turned up for the Medal from all quarters of the globe, are no different from other club golfers, in that the handicaps of practically none of them bear any relation to fact.

It nearly always happens that one dark horse slips through the committee's tightly meshed net, and this year was no exception, the hero this time being a local doctor who did 82–15–67 and will doubtless find himself playing off scratch for the next fifteen years. Apart from this, however, I noted only three net 72s, six 74s, five 75s, and twelve 76s. There were a hundred and twenty at '80 and over' and fifty-eight at '84 and over'. Those who got round in 84 could not play to 20 or even 30. Nor does the list include the innumerable 'no returns' who might not have played to 50. It all seems to confirm my theory that the number of golfers who can really play to their handicaps, all holed out and from the Medal tees, is infinitesimal.

Two performances at St Andrews call, as I think you will agree, for special comment. To set the scene I should perhaps say that on Wednesday with a stiff cold wind blowing against on the way out, the par for me personally for the first five holes was 5, 5, 4, 5, 5. The fact that I started 6, 6, 5, 7, 6, and then got in a gorse bush and walked in is immaterial.

Rear-Admiral Benson is eighty-one and a quarter years old. He carries, at the 'trail arms' position, a patent club-container built in 1893, with wooden legs which prop it up as you set it down. Five clubs—the driver, the wooden cleek, the short spoon, the spade mashie and the 'skibo', which is a sort of mashie-niblick—rest side by side in metal clips. A wooden mallet putter is housed in a plastic tube at the side.

In these conditions a renowned ex-Walker-Cup player took 91. The Admiral, carrying his own clubs, holed the Old Course from the Medal tees in 88, and without a single 6 in the last nine. Deducting his handicap of sixteen—and how many golfers of eighty-one can play to that?—he finished equal second with a net 72. Jack Nicklaus, who is twenty-five, recently did a 64 in the Masters Tournament. Will he, I wonder, be able to do an 88 at 81?

At Pine Valley, near Philadelphia, which to the indifferent player is probably the world's most punishing golf course, they have a tradition that, never mind how many you take, you hole out to the bitter end and admit it. I am glad that this does not apply on Medal days at St Andrews, for too many faces, including my own, would be too red at the end of the day. On the other hand one cannot but lift one's hat to the character who on Wednesday did indeed, I gather, soldier on to the end and returned a card of 154−25=129.

His figures deserve a wider public than merely the handicapping committee (who must surely put him up to twenty-six next year) and were, I am assured, as follows:

9, 9, 10, 8, 11, 9, 13, 4, 7=80
7, 5, 9, 6, 11, 7, 12, 9, 8=74

I thought that the Old Course (or what I saw of it) was a tremendous credit to the links superintendent, Mr Campbell. Nevertheless it is a fact that those parts of the fairways from which second or third shots are habitually played look pock-marked and ghastly. This is the fault not of Mr Campbell or his staff, nor of the golfers, who meticulously put back the divots they have hacked out of the sacred turf, but of a comparatively small number of evil-looking crows, each patrolling its own 'beat' and picking out the divots as soon as they are replaced. As a result a number of men are perpetually and expensively employed filling in thousands of divot marks with a mixture of grass seed and sand, unsightly to the eye and impossible to play off.

I appear to be the first person to have had the brilliant inspiration that it might be both cheaper and more satisfactory to dispense with the crows and thereafter with the men who follow them round with the grass seed. The crows do, it is true, assist with the corporation's rubbish dump at the end of the Jubilee course, but there are sufficient gulls to handle this municipal chore on their own and we could well afford, in the time-honoured phrase, to 'stone the crows'. How exactly you stone a crow I have never quite gathered, but clearly it can, and in this case should, be done.

Perhaps one of those bird-scaring apparatuses which go off with a bang every minute or so might meet the case. It conjures up, if nothing else, a splendid vision of members attempting short putts at the precise moment of detonation and eventually being turned into nervous wrecks, unable to play until the next bang had gone off.

The only trouble is that on so many days the explosion would be inaudible either to man or bird on account of the Lightning aeroplanes now based at Leuchars. To see the four of them flying in formation at several hundred miles an hour is a noble sight, but the young fellow who at 4.30 on Tuesday spent some minutes seeing how long he could screech round and round the sky on one wing-tip, as though tearing off colossal strips of celestial calico, may be interested to know that conversation, even by yelling at the top of one's voice, was rendered impossible on the Old Course, especially on the more distant parts whose sense of remoteness and tranquility has so long been their special charm.

ARNOLD PALMER'S 'HAPPY CIRCLE'

I often suspect that little is to be learned by people like myself from instructional books on golf by people like Palmer and Nicklaus, for the simple reason that they cannot possibly know, fortunately for them, what it feels like to be me. They therefore recommend me to get myself into positions in which high-speed photography shows them to get themselves, little knowing that if I did so I should be taken straight to the infirmary.

As an avid reader of autobiographies, however, in which without any trouble on your own part you can live through the successes, disappointments and adventures of another man's life in a couple of hours, I always welcome those parts of their books which tell me of the life they lead, and reveal, whether they mean to or not, what manner of man they really are. For this reason I am grateful to an American friend for sending me Arnold Palmer's new book which, despite its title, *My Game and Yours*, is more about Palmer than how to swing a golf club.

I doubt whether any great player has so thoroughly enjoyed and loved playing the game as Palmer. He first swing a club at the age of four and was 'completely hooked on golf' by the time he was seven or eight. At eleven he started caddying at the Latrobe Club in Pennsylvania where his father was, and is, professional, and eventually he became caddiemaster—the worst, his father said, that he had ever experienced, since the moment there was no one about he locked up the shop and adjourned to the practice ground. 'You've heard of vicious circles,' he writes. 'Mine was a happy circle. The more I played the better I got, and the better I got the more I wanted to play.'

When he had already become a top-class amateur, he beat Bobby Sweeny in the final of the 1954 US Amateur—a match which, happening to be in the neighbourhood, I remember watching—and some friends lured him down to Pine Valley, where, as you may know, all manner of bets will be laid against the newcomer, offensive to his dignity and almost inevitably painful to his pocket. In Palmer's case the wager was that he should receive a hundred dollars for every stroke under 72 and should pay a hundred for every stroke over 80. Starting with a ten-yard putt for a 5 at the par-4 1st, he holed Pine Valley at first sight in 68, thereby winning $400, plus another $400 on the side.

'It was a sucker bet,' he says, 'but I was young and in love and nothing could scare me.' He blued the lot on an engagement ring.

Palmer was due to visit Britain for the Walker Cup match but he turned pro instead. In his first tournament he failed to qualify for the last day, went out on the town and arrived next morning to ask her parents for his lady-friend's hand in marriage—which, in view of the fact that he had not yet earned a penny in his new career and, further-more, had omitted to shave, they not unnaturally refused. The pair therefore eloped and have lived happily ever after.

One of Palmer's finest performances was in the 1962 Open Champion-ship at Troon, not merely his winning of it but his handling of a course some parts of which, by American championship standards, would have been considered unfit for play. Having said that a golf course itself can get you mad, if you let it, he writes: 'The course at Troon was too unpredictable. There had been a long drought and the fairways were baked into iron. And Troon is so full of ridges and humps that there was absolutely no telling, with the ground as hard as it was, where any shot would end up. One day, on the 15th, I hit what I think was probably the finest drive of my life, long and absolutely square right down the centre of the fairway on the exact line I had planned. Yet when I got to the ball I found that it had bounced all the way off the fairway and into a thick tangle of downhill rough.

'Things like this can bother you all right, but you don't have to let them get you really down. When I played my first practice round over Troon, I decided right then and there that I wasn't going to let myself get locked into a life-and-death struggle with the course. Sure I was going to get some bad bounces. But nobody had planned the drought; nobody was to blame. And the course was as baked for the other players as for me; everybody else was going to get bad bounces too. I decided that I would keep the ball right in the centre, as nearly as I could, to allow a maximum leeway for a bounce to either side.

'The 12th hole at Troon was a particular monster; it is ordinarily a par-5 but for the tournament it had been converted into a terrifying 460-yard par-4. Some of the players took one look at it and threw up their hands. I myself decided to treat it with respect, but not with fear. In my own mind I would regard it as a sort of par-4$\frac{1}{2}$. I would play it to take a 5 if necessary, and sort of hope for a 4 as a bonus. Instead of using a driver off the tee, risking the heavy and almost unplayable rough that lay on either side, I used a 3-wood and some-times a 1-iron. This left me a difficult 1-iron or 2-iron to the green, but that was the price I had to pay for safety; and I made up my mind to pay the price carefully. Well, in my four cracks at number 12 I scored a 5, two 4s and a 3. And I won the tournament.'

All the great golfers of the past have had their quota of fans and admirers, but none have inspired such galleries as have come to be known as 'Arnie's Army'. I have more than once been caught up in

F

this army myself and have felt their sense not merely of hero-worship but of an almost personal affection for a man they have never met and probably never will.

Sometimes the pressure of it all gets him momentarily down.

'When I have to start a tournament after posing all the morning for photographs that an advertising agency needs for one of the companies in which I have an interest; and some newspapermen have been interviewing me during the breaks; and I get word that my lawyer has been trying to get hold of me on the phone; and there's a wire at the golf course asking me to take part in a charity television show— when all these things happen, as they often do, I sometimes long for the good old days when nobody knew me from Adam and all I had to do was practise and play golf.

'But then I get a few days' break between tournaments and I step into my airplane and fly home, something that I couldn't have done until I became successful at golf, something that none of yesterday's pros could afford to do. It's a plane that golf bought me, and to a family which would never have had its present comforts and opportunities without golf.'

Palmer has taken more out of golf than any man in the game's history. It is in keeping with his character that he should also have put more back.

HARD WORDS ON THE COMMON

Continuity, it has been said, is the essence of English history, and it was in this spirit that teams representing fifty clubs have just assembled to contend for a trophy celebrating the hundredth year of continuous golf on or beside Wimbledon Common. I do not know how many clubs in the world enjoy the prefix 'Royal', but at any rate no fewer than twenty-nine were represented at Royal Wimbledon yesterday, including Hong Kong, Salisbury, Nairobi, Calcutta, Melbourne, Montreal, Sydney, Hobart and Bombay.

What a fantastic picture this would have seemed to the enthusiasts of the London Scottish Rifle Volunteers when they first started knocking balls about on the Common while waiting their turn on the range! Their first headquarters were at Mrs Doggett's cottage by the windmill, but soon after their club had been formed, with that fiery and formidable figure, Lord Elcho, MP, as President, they were allotted quarters in the iron shooting-house. Here the highlight of the year was the annual match against Blackheath—presumably, with the exception of Westward Ho!, the only golf club in England at the time—the play being 'Fourteen a side. Man against man. Three rounds of the ground: twenty-one holes. To count holes, not strokes,' to be followed by dinner at the Dog and Fox.

Wimbledon was the scene of the first University match in 1878 and it was held there continuously until 1892. This, too, was played by holes up or down—not subtracting the loser's total and simply giving the winner's margin of victory but allowing credit where credit was due—e.g., 1886: *Oxford 37, Cambridge* [I am happy to see] *39*.

Bernard Darwin, who played in the match in 1895-6-7, sometimes used to intrigue us with tales of those different days. Cambridge, it seems, to play Wimbledon, used to make their way from King's Cross on the morning of play in a knife-board horse carriage, and returned with W. T. Linskill, the 'founder of Cambridge golf', sleeping it peacefully off in the boot.

I often feel that, were they not, so to speak, private property, one could produce some splendid reading with a selection from the suggestion books of golf clubs. Lord Brabazon's at Sandwich 'that the water in the bunkers at the 13th be changed' would, of course, rank high in the list, but so, I suspect, would some in the earlier days at Wimbledon.

Connoisseurs and critics of the sanitary arrangements at golfing events today will approve of the suggestion by Mr Faithfull and Professor Chalmers 'that a kettle be purchased for the club room at the Iron House, so that members who prefer washing in hot water to washing in cold may be able to gratify their legitimate desire'. They may also care to note that to visit the single convenience at the Iron House cost a penny a time—so perhaps we are not so badly off after all. The suggestion to end all suggestions also figures in the London Scottish book: 'Suggested that the committee take a look at some of these suggestions.'

One of the principal thorns in the committee's flesh through the medium of the suggestion book was the great Dr Laidlaw Purves. Golf was a small world in the seventies and eighties, and the worthy doctor loomed large in it. He was a principal founder of the Royal St George's Club at Sandwich—his portrait hangs on the wall both there and over the dining-room hatch at Royal Wimbledon—and only the other day I was reading the impassioned harangue he delivered to a group of ladies who were in the process of forming themselves into the Ladies Golf Union.

These were the days also when the golfer was a more peppery and outspoken character than he is permitted to be today—though the legend of the apoplectic Colonel swearing in the bunker certainly dies hard. One Saturday, playing in the monthly medal, Dr Purves and Mr David Lamb fell into dispute regarding the marking of the latter's card.

'Taking each party's case on his own representation,' the committee reported, 'the committee consider that there was no occasion for such hasty inferences on both sides, or such loss of temper as was evidently displayed on one. Dr Purves ought to have stated his objection before the ball was played, not after the hole had been played out. On the other hand the committee are of opinion that nothing that Dr Purves said was capable of the construction put upon it, or warranted the strong epithet admitted to have been used by Mr Lamb.'

In 1871, when their club was only six years old, the London Scottish Rifle Volunteers, out of the goodness of their hearts, opened it to 'outsiders'. All unwittingly they had let a cuckoo, in the shape of hordes of civilian English, into their little nest, and, struggle though they might, they were in the end to be pushed out. By 1878 the young cuckoo, outweighing the foster-parent in the ratio of five to one, was now clamouring for the whole family to be moved to a more commodious nest, Lord Elcho and other 'Scotchmen' (as they then described themselves, in a term which for some extraordinary reason is now regarded as a deadly insult) vigorously dissenting.

Few propositions are calculated more surely to divide golfers among themselves than the suggestion that they should move to new and more comfortable premises, and so it proved with the London Scottish.

The minutes of some of the meetings ran to fifty-four printed pages, and some of the reports would do no discredit to Hansard today.

Mr Guy Pym: I consider Lord Elcho's explanation most unsatisfactory [hear! hear! and hisses]. He has made a statement which, with his Parliamentary experience of some forty years, I feal certain he must be very much ashamed of [hear! hear! applause and hisses].

Major Flood Page: I rise to order.

Colonel Moncrieff: Kindly sit down.

Major Page: I rise to order [interruption].

Lord Elcho: I think Major Page has a right to reply.

Major Page: I think Mr Pym ought not to say to any member in this room that he has done anything to be ashamed of . . . [loud applause and hisses].

Colonel Moncrieff: I daresay Mr Pym will withdraw the word 'ashamed' [cries of 'Oh, no!' hisses and interruptions]. Gentlemen, I must remind you that we are a meeting of gentlemen [loud cries of hear! hear!] and therefore I think those gentlemen who are hissing had better be quiet.

So the two agreed to disagree. The Corps members retired in a huff, calling themselves the 'London Scottish' Golf Club: the rest moved to new premises and called themselves the London Scottish Golf Club—without the inverted commas.

For many, many years now peace has reigned on the Common, both among those who still play on it in their red coats and those who play at what is now Royal Wimbledon. It only remains to hope that all who gathered there yesterday from all parts of the world had an enjoyable day, and that in a hundred years time their grandsons and great-grandsons will be gathering there again to celebrate the second hundred years.

FLAT OUT FOR CHAMPIONS

Two of the world's greatest experts, each from his own side of the fence, having recently given their views on the subject brings me to the question of the ideal championship course, and, if there is such a thing, could you and I play on it with any degree of pleasure too?

The experts in question are Arnold Palmer, writing in the American magazine *Esquire* and Robert Trent Jones, who has set out his ideas in the Journal of the US Golf Association. Mr Jones, a native of Ince, nr Liverpool, from which he was withdrawn at an early age to the New World, is probably the world's most prolific golf architect, simultaneously designing from his drawing-board in New York courses as far apart as Spain and Hawaii.

Indeed, he has made such a good thing out of it that he was able once to entertain me to dinner at Maxim's in Paris, at the height of the American tourist season, without flinching at the bill.

Each seems to think it possible to extend the champions on courses which would still give pleasure to the club player, but, after seeing so many players make nonsense of the last two holes at Birkdale, I begin to wonder. The operative word is 'extend'. Hitting the ball flat out is one of the joys of golf and the champions should not, in my opinion, be deprived of it.

If, however, they reach holes of 513 and 510 yards nonchalantly with a 5-iron, or even less, it is clear that nothing short of 800 yards will give them our own equivalent of a long hole—the kind of which the caddie observed, 'It'll take three dam' good shots to get up in two today, sir.' I wonder, for instance, how many times Jack Nicklaus in a whole year of tournament golf takes a brassie for his second? Half a dozen? I doubt it.

Palmer's ideal course is long, 7,080 yards in fact, 'because golfers today learn to hit hard and long before they learn any other aspect of the game'. Like most people's ideal course it has four short holes, ten par-4s and four par-5s—'long and lean', physically reachable in two but with so narrow a target as to make it not worth while going for the green.

I was brought up on the theory that the size of the green should vary in proportion with the length of shot with which you approach it. An example is the 8th hole at Pine Valley, where the second shot is no more than an eighty-yard pitch. The green, as you play this little shot to it, seems to shrink to a tiny, microscopic hump surrounded entirely by sand and I remember being told how Roger Wethered—I hope I do him no injustice—plied his way to and fro for an 11.

Current American practice, as exemplified both in Palmer's 'perfect course' and those which I have seen of Trent Jones's, is to make very big, undulating greens, each with anything up to five 'pin positions', some of them fantastically difficult, so that you are either hoping to get down in one putt or trying to avoid taking three. I was about to write how little this appealed to me by comparison with simply adjusting the size of the target, when I realized that it is the crafty pin-positions which 'make' the Old Course at St Andrews.

'Rough,' says Trent Jones, 'will be very much a part of the penalty for misplaced shots in the Open Championship.' This is certainly the policy of the USGA, who, two or three years beforehand, decide upon the precise height and extent of the long grass and often end up by leaving many of the competitors howling for mercy.

'There is no rough,' says Palmer, on the other hand. 'The grass off the fairways, instead of receiving the care of the green-keeper, will be allowed to grow for itself but not to a height which would interfere with play. I've long felt that high rough is unfair because it does not collect the same penalty from each man.' He has, instead, trees, short and tall, dense and thin, and most of the rest of the trouble, he says, can be solved with 'a good shot, or educated gambling'.

Palmer's views on bunkers are novel and, as it seems to me, intelligent. His fairway bunkers—which do not worry the club golfer since he simply does not reach them—are 'shallow', with lips only about three feet high, so as to allow a long iron, perfectly hit, to carry out of the bunker and reach the green. Round the green, however, he uses 'Scottish' traps (an expression new to me, this), from which the ball 'must be struck so that it gets airborne quickly and only the sense of feel of the great trap shot will enable a player to get his ball close to the pin, since its point of landing almost surely will be out of his sight'.

Though one can think of many historic water hazards in this country, they tend to be the exception, whereas, in American country-club golf, ponds, lakes or creeks are almost the rule. Palmer's course has plenty of water and most of it, I notice, is on the right. Trent Jones is kinder-hearted. When the Canada Cup tournament was played at Dorado Beach, in Puerto Rico, he was designing a further eighteen holes and took me round to inspect them in an electric buggy. Beside many of the holes he was causing great pits to be dug, destined in the course of nature to fill with water. Nearly all, I observed, were on the left. He is a slicer, too!

As golf balls, according to the makers' advertisements, go farther and farther and Nicklaus reduces the great Augusta National to a drive and a pitch, I envisage eventually a 'world-championship course' to end all championship courses, probably in the Californian so-called desert, which is in fact so fertile that you have only to 'sow the seed, apply the water, and jump back'.

This course will be 15,000 yards long, so designed as to be capable of indefinite extension to accommodate later increases in the length of the ball, and the par-5 holes will measure 900–1,000 yards, thus giving Nicklaus the unparalleled experience of taking a long iron for his third.

The players will ride round in atomically propelled carts and alongside each hole I see a continuous moving pavement for the spectators, who will be able to step off from time to time for refreshment or even, by missing the play at two or three holes, to take in a movie.

The Press, it need hardly be said, will follow by fully licensed helicopter.

'SEANACHIE' IMPRESSARIO

One of my oldest cronies in the world of golf is Fred Corcoran. Roughing it, as I am at the moment of writing, in the autumn sunshine at Gleneagles, I cannot lay hands on a dictionary, but am pretty certain that 'crony' must be the right word, since on two occasions Fred and I have sat up talking in the Prince of Wales Hotel at Southport throughout the whole of the night and this seems to be rather the sort of thing one expects Cronies to do.

Fred's father, an Irish immigrant to Boston in the days when the 'Situations Vacant' Columns still carried the line 'No Irish need apply', never let the world trap him into regular employment. He was, instead, a 'seanachie'—in other words, he lived by telling stories, mostly to visitors whom he induced to accompany him on a guided tour of Harvard.

His son, Fred, inherited similar characteristics and now in a book called *Unplayable Lies*, which I hope will be published over here, he turns 'seanachie' himself and reflects upon a lifetime spent as an impressario in the centre of the American sporting scene, with special reference to golf.

Corcoran brought the 1937 and 1953 Ryder Cup teams to England and enjoyed, if that is the appropriate term, the position of tournament manager to the PGA—a quarrelsome lot, it would appear—from 1936 to 1947. He founded the Ladies PGA, has managed Sam Snead for the best part of thirty years, and runs the Canada Cup, now known as the World Cup. In other words, he has seen it all.

Like so many of the best-known figures in American golf, Fred Corcoran started as a caddie ('See what it has done for that Ouimet boy,' said his mother in 1913) and can claim the double distinction of having been, at twelve, the country's youngest caddie master and of having thrown a golf ball in the air for the great Annie ('get-your-gun') Oakley. She stood with her back turned, then whipped round and hit it in mid-air.

When one thinks of the huge scoreboards of today, to say nothing of the 'animated Location Board' used at the Ryder Cup at Birkdale, it is interesting to read: 'When I travelled to England with the American Walker Cup team in 1934, the "scoreboard" at Prestwick for the British Amateur consisted of a sheet of ordinary letterhead stationery tacked to the starter's table, fluttering in the wind. The best you could wring out of it in the way of information was such tight-lipped messages as "Guildford 2 and 1" written in lead pencil.' Long before this, Corcoran had revolutionized scoring in America with multicoloured chalks and descriptive details and may fairly be termed the 'father' of the modern scoreboard.

One turns instinctively, of course, to his recollections of Walter Hagen, who 'lived the life lesser men dream about as they plod back and forth between their offices and the subway' and 'hated to go to bed because sleeping seemed like such a waste of time'. The picture of Hagen flashing through life with champagne bubbling out of his ears is, says Corcoran, a false one. 'The Hagen of his golden years took excellent care of himself. He was the world's champion hider of drinks. Walter always had a full glass in his hand. But after the ball was over, the sweeper would find a dozen drinks lined up behind the piano where Hagen had slyly secreted them during the revels.'

Hagen was a great one for 'laying off' at regular intervals. 'These players today,' he once said, 'they just don't seem to understand you have to put your clubs away sometimes and do something else for a while.' One wonders what he would have thought of Gary Player's recent schedule: Saturday, Wentworth; Monday and Tuesday, Ohio; Thursday, Australia! When Hagen came over in 1929 to lose his historic challenge match with Archie Compston by 18 and 17, he 'had not,' according to Corcoran, 'swung a club in weeks.'

After a few holes Hagen seemed to chuck his hand in, apparently unconcerned about the outcome. 'If you're going to be beaten,' he said, 'it doesn't make any difference if you're beaten by one hole or ten. It was a wonderful chance to get a lot of bad shots out of my system at once.' Two weeks later Hagen spreadeagled the field at Muirfield to win his fourth, and probably finest, Open Championship.

On the aeroplane from Augusta to Atlanta after the Masters tournament last year, I sat next to a positively enormous man whom I recognized as Ralph Guldahl. In the late thirties he had been the Hogan of his day. He had won two consecutive US Opens, three consecutive Western Opens, the Masters, and a host of lesser titles. I wondered why we never seemed to hear much about him thereafter and Corcoran now reveals the answer. Poor Guldahl, he went to bed one night unchallengeably the greatest golfer in America—and woke up to find he could not hit his hat. His game had vanished and he never found it again. He wound up in a small club in California. A strange and rather pathetic tale.

Snead, on the other hand, though he has never won the US Open— he once had a 5 to win and before he knew what he was doing had taken 8—has been a consistently great golfer for thirty years, the only one, says Corcoran, who has won a million and saved two million. Snead has one great regret in life. He feels very deeply, and in my opinion quite unnecessarily, about being bald—which is why he never appears in public, even at a prizegiving, without his hat. On one occasion Corcoran was woken each morning by thumping noises from Snead's room next door. It transpired that the great golfer was walking on his hands to make his hair grow. Someone had told him that a rush of blood to the scalp would do the trick!

Corcoran tells an interesting story illustrating the genius of Bing Crosby by comparison with today's 'pop' singers. At the end of a day's filming by Crosby the two of them walked down the street to a sound studio where Crosby was due to make a recording. 'The place was empty except for the band and the Andrews Sisters and Jerome Kern, the songwriter. Bing and the girls hummed the song over a couple of times, then cut the record with the band. Then they hummed it again and made another cut. That was it. The whole business took no more than ten minutes and the record sold in millions. It was a song called "Don't Fence Me In".'

No one can be better qualified than Fred Corcoran to give an opinion as to why British, indeed European, professionals cannot match up to their American rivals, and he puts it down, rather disappointingly, simply to hard work. In the Canada Cup in Paris two years ago, he says, Palmer and Nicklaus hit more balls in practice than the other thirty-two teams put together. The rest were 'enjoying their prerogatives as travelling representatives of the leisured class'.

Yet he also recalls Hagen watching Byron Nelson hitting a barrage of flawless iron shots and saying, 'What a shame to waste those great shots on the practice tee! What are they doing out there anyway? Those guys already know how to hit a golf ball. They don't have to do that.'

I am all in favour of other people working hard. On the other hand instinct tells me that, if my life had been cast as that of a professional golfer, I should have been more likely to range myself with Hagen on the sideline, enjoying the prerogatives of the leisured class.

THE STROLLING MILLIONAIRES

I am sometimes accused, possibly with justice, of paying less attention than I should to amateur golfers and too much to the itinerant professionals who are flown continuously round the world, picking up in the process so much money that some of them even begin giving it away. Yet it is excusable, if in a way regrettable, that the activities of these fellows, who largely through the medium of television have become nationally recognizable figures to millions who never set foot on a golf course, should prove of such compulsive interest.

They are in a sense the pop singers of the sporting world, in that suddenly, over a mere ten years or so, they find themselves showered with fantastic riches for doing something which is in itself entirely unnecessary and which their fathers for a comparative pittance did just as well before them—and, if you don't believe the last part, see Open Championship, Royal St George's, thirty-one years ago, when Cotton started 67, 65, to say nothing of a 66 in the qualifying.

The envy naturally engendered by all this among hard-working hacks like myself is tempered by the thought that these millionaire propellers of the golf ball are extremely good fellows, and this goes especially for the amiable Tony Lema, who was with us for a day or two last week on his way round a world-wide hotel chain, accompanied by an equally amiable young man, William Bossard, a 2-handicap player from Akron, Ohio, who had won this global tour in Lema's company as a prize in a golf tournament.

Poor Mr Bossard, incidentally, was at once deprived by the hard-hearted US Golf Association of his amateur status, and this will raise a nice point in the minds of us all. For exactly how much would you relinquish your own amateur standing and never play in a competition again? For a trip round the world with Lema? Possibly. For the £10,000 won by Harold Henning for doing a hole in one in the Esso tournament at Moor Park? Instantly. For myself, I am not sure that I would not relinquish it simply on the basis that I need never play in a competition again.

Lema, Open Champion of 1964, appeals as an essentially 'human' golfer. Now in his early thirties,* he did not, like Palmer and Nicklaus, go straight from college into golf via a spell in the amateur ranks but worked as general bottle-washer in San Francisco Canneries and then did two years' service in the Marines, including Korea, before getting his first golf as an assistant pro. In tournament golf, too, he came up the hard way and it took him 'a cheque-book full of fines and a lot

* Alas, he and his charming wife were killed in an air crash on their way to a tournament, a great loss to the golfing scene.

of temper tantrums', as he puts it, before he realized that playing golf was thirty per cent physical and seventy per cent mental, and that 'lose control of the mental side and you are only thirty per cent a golfer'. Once, after hitting his ball into a ditch, he threw the club in after it, then the rest of his clubs and the bag, and, if his caddie had not moved pretty sharply, he would almost certainly have gone in too.

Now Lema is on top of the world, earning well over $100,000 a year and enjoying every moment of it, the only cloud on his horizon being what usually passes as 'tennis elbow' in his right arm—and the thought that one tiny muscle could put paid to everything. One hopes that he will soon recover, not merely for himself but because he has just signed a contract to play with British clubs all over the world and may therefore do our export trade a good turn.

Another reason is that he told me he proposed in a year or two to publish another book, not about how to play golf (he is himself a perfectly 'simple' player like, say, Peter Thomson or Peter Allis) but about his life, follies and fortunes, or, as he called the first one, published here last year, his *Inside Story*.

I find Lema's attitude—and gratitude—to golf most appealing. 'Where else,' he wrote in his first book, 'can a man advance on pure and simple ability, where only scores, not office, politics, or friends in the right places count? What sport could yield an annual income of half a million dollars to a man of thirty-four like Arnold Palmer . . . or 100,000 to a former cannery-worker of thirty like me?' At the time he wrote this he had yet to win the British Open, or the first prize of £12,500 in the Carling Tournament.

In the latter Lema was caught by Palmer, who came charging from four shots behind to draw level with three to play, but Palmer it was that cracked, while Lema from that moment hit nothing but perfect shots to win. The pressure under which such golf is played—at an average rate of only four holes per hour—has broken twenty men for every one who has survived it. Golf, to Lema's mind, is 'not a game designed to be played under this sort of pressure. It is a game for a pleasant day, with only a quiet group of friends to play with you and no pressure but the satisfaction of turning in a good score.'

What is the secret? 'A good teaching professional,' says Lema, 'can teach a young man to hit a golf ball with a stick pretty near perfectly every time. But how do you teach that man to hit that tiny ball with a long whippy stick when 15,000 people are jammed around him like a crowd at a six-alarm fire, when several million eyes are peering at him on television and when a quarter of a million dollars is riding directly or indirectly on the next shot he hits?'

The answer is as simple as can be. The survivors who have learned to take the pressure of playing for these fantastically high stakes have learned to do it by doing it. The rest fall by the wayside.

'It is astonishing,' wrote Lema, 'when someone as highly strung as Gary Player is able to win a major championship. . . .' Player at that time had won two. Since then he has added the US Open and the Piccadilly Match-Play tournament in which, ironically enough, he beat Lema from seven down with seventeen to play. He has also on a shortish course at Adelaide had 62s in the first and third rounds—the second rather superior to the first, he thought, since he 'did not falter over the last few holes'.

ANYONE LEND ME £100,000?

Will any gentle reader lend me a hundred thousand pounds, or maybe, while we are about it, a couple? If so, I shall reply to the following advertisement, which will have intrigued all who saw it in the agony column of *The Times*:

> GOLFER'S DREAM—180 acres land available, sufficient for two 18-hole courses with planning permission granted in beautiful West Hertfordshire countryside: situated about 25 miles from London, the site has easy access from there by road (3 miles from M1 Motorway) and rail (1 mile from station on new electrified London Midland Region line).

Long experience of golf clubs convinces me that there is no administration to touch that of the benevolent dictator. This is a role in which I strongly fancy myself and it is tantalizing to think that only the shortage of a few tens of thousands stands between me and the fulfilling of so long-standing an ambition. My model would be that of 'Aber'—the late J. F. Abercromby—who reigned before the war first at Coombe Hill and later, when despite the difference in our ages I came to know him well, at Addington.

'Aber' had a lean, rather hawk-like countenance, and a green velour pork-pie hat, which, together with the wooden putter which he invariably carried on his walks round the course, was almost his trademark. Some of us younger ones derived much innocent fun from getting behind him at the bar and muttering, just loudly enough for him to hear, about its being 'such a pity about the conditions of the greens' and 'only last week, I believe, four more members left for Addington Palace'. Eventually the old boy, unable to stand any more, would whip round, only to find that his leg had been pulled again. Good schoolboy stuff, and it never failed.

'Aber' stood positively no nonsense from anybody. One simple remark, which I was lucky enough to overhear, explained everything. 'Where's the suggestion book?' an aggrieved member asked the steward. 'Aber' turned and fixed the man with a baleful eye. Prodding him slowly with a bony forefinger, then pointing to himself, he said, '*I'm* the suggestion book.'

He was, I suspect, the greatest golf architect of them all, and it is with no disrespect to his colleagues of today that I say that I should have turned to him to design my new course in Hertfordshire. When he first dived into the woods and bracken and brambles at Addington, they were so thick that he and his assistant could keep in touch only

by blowing whistles. The instinct by which he designed the Old
Course 'blind'—and, I have been assured, with no major changes
required when the scrub was cleared away—never ceases to astonish me.

When he wanted to make the new course, they assured him that
the ground could never be drained. It may well have needed only
this to make him determined to go ahead. He not only did so but
created what was to become widely quoted as probably the best
inland course in the country. It is now a council estate.

Such a ghastly decision, and one which, incidently, cost the rate-
payers of Croydon rather more than £120,000, would probably not
be made today, now that golf has become a game which the majority
of voters not only want to enjoy but can also afford. The New course
at Addington, in the heart of a dense population, could today have
been giving untold pleasure as the best public course in the world.

Now none other than the Minister responsible for sport, Mr Denis
Howell, MP, has said, 'As a matter of sport policy I wish to encourage
golf, particularly in ways which will bring it within reach of as many
people as possible,' and it is as heartening now as it would have been
unbelievable fifteen years ago that 180 acres of Hertfordshire should
be planned as a golf course.

The advertisement is, I think, optimistic in saying 'sufficient for two
eighteen-hole courses', and my plan will be, when I get the money,
to have one eighteen-hole course, one par-3—not necessarily either
nine or eighteen holes, but as many as we can fit in—a covered driving-
and practice-range, and two exceptionally fine eighteen-hole practice-
greens.

Players would be forbidden to use their own practice balls but would
hire them from the professional, then leave them to be picked up by a
machine. This involves a certain amount of faith in human nature.
When the pro at a very well-known and respectable London club
started hiring out practice balls, clearly identified with broad yellow
rings, they were being offered for sale in a local shop within a week!

I expect to see a spectacular rise in the number of par-3 courses—
which are after all full-sized courses, minus fourteen drives—and
anticipate that mine will be immensely popular, especially on summer
evenings and Sunday afternoons. Only the other day I happened to
drive by the new par-3 course designed by Henry Cotton in the park
at Farnham, Surrey. So far as I could see, every tee and green had
four people on it and you could not have squeezed in another player
anywhere on the course.

I shall probably have no rough at all—none at any rate that you
can lose your ball in—and I doubt whether I shall have any sand
bunkers, which after all are no more than a feeble attempt to imitate

the original linksland golf among the sand dunes beside the sea. Instead, you will find a wayward shot among or behind flowering shrubs or trees, on which I shall have spent about £5,000, or obstructed by mounds or dips around the green.

Only those who have seen the lovely Ailsa course at Turnberry as part of a wartime airfield and as it is today can appreciate what can be achieved by a bulldozer and an intelligent driver.

There will be three tees in constant use at every hole on my main course, the middle one within a few paces of the previous green, and the greens as a general principle will vary in size in direct ratio to the length of shot with which you approach them.

Women will be delighted to know that they will at all times have exactly equal rights with men, including that of paying the same subscription, and I shall invite several to sit on the committee—a body of which, as benevolent dictator, I shall take no notice except in so far as it takes tedious work off my own shoulders.

No cash will be taken in the club. A chit system will operate, everything being signed for, as in America, and any member who has not spent what I deem to be a reasonable amount in the club each month will be billed for it anyway. The only exception to the 'no-cash' rule will be the six one-armed bandits, the profits of which will be voted by the committee towards the benevolent dictator's Benevolent Fund.

ROBBERY WITHOUT VIOLENCE

The Limerick Golf Club, which is the second oldest in Eire, is to celebrate its seventy-fifth anniversary this year with a series of matches in which four Ryder Cup players, Christy O'Connor, Peter Alliss, George Will and David Thomas, will each take on the best ball of three of Ireland's leading amateurs. This unique competition, they feel, should arouse controversy concerning the result. In myself it arouses not so much controversy as memories that remain poignant and painful despite the passing of many a long year.

I have recounted before, but may be permitted briefly to do so again because of its particular relevance, how Archie Compston, having seen the Cambridge team of which I had the honour to be captain, sat on the fender at Coombe Hill, pronounced us a 'bunch of lousy golfers', and declared that he could beat any three of us. W. H. Bermingham, who was our longest hitter and the only man I have ever seen before or since to play golf in pince-nez, N. A. Keith and I took up the challenge. I must say I thought we were on to a good thing and acted accordingly. I have been wondering what went wrong ever since.

One thing was that Compston had craftily set the tees—it was in winter—in such a way that there were six holes which he could reach in two and we couldn't, though Bermingham could get somewhere near. I hope I do the latter no injustice after all these years in recalling that at those moments when his length was vital to our cause he was inclined to drive into the woods. Compston holed the course in 68 and we lost on the last green. What had gone wrong?

All three of us had handicaps of scratch or one. I am the first to admit that the scratch man of that time was by no means the fearsome player he has to be today, nor were we the equal of most of the top Irish amateurs who will play at Limerick, though I daresay we could then have given most of them a run for their money. All the same, three of us ought surely to have been able to do the great man in, even on his home course. It was a long time before I found the answer.

It is that, with players of fairly level ability, three are better than two only to the extent to which the third beats the better ball of the other two. In other words, how many holes is the third man going to win outright from his two companions? He may well play perfectly well, yet never win a hole. When he gets a two, for instance, one of the others gets one too. So, in effect, he has proved valueless. To make it worse, he may in fact win a hole from his two partners—a 4, say, against two 5s—but, even so, lose it to a 3 by the enemy.

Of course, one cannot in advance nominate which of the three is the 'third man' but, if it should happen that any of the three fails to win a hole against the other two, then those two would have been as good as three. This was the trap that Compston had laid for us and it worked, for it so happened that one of us did fail to improve on the other two and so, in effect, he played only two of us instead of three, as a result of which I had to sell my poor old Morris Cowley and it rankles still.

Nevertheless, three surely ought to beat one, however distinguished the one may be. It occurred to me to seek a further example from the *Golf Illustrated* Gold Vase at Sunningdale, and through the courtesy of the Editor of that journal, Mr Tom Scott, I have before me a maze of figures relating to the winner, Clive Clark, matched against what we took to be a good representative trio—the amateur champion, Michael Bonallack, Walker Cup player Rodney Foster and a rising hope of Sunningdale, John Tullis. Foster and Tullis, I will reveal, finished equal sixth with 145, Bonallack equal ninth with 146. Could the three of them combined, do you think, beat Clark, who won with 139?

This particular example shows that three do tend to beat one but that it still would not be wise to invest too confidently in the result. Over the Old Course the three of them beat Clark by 2 and 1. Over the New they beat him 3 and 2. On both courses Tullis proved to be the number-one man of the trio, beating the other two three times on the Old and four times on the New. Bonallack and Foster each won two holes on the Old but qualified jointly as 'third man' on the New by influencing the result at only one hole. Yet every instinct would have led one to believe that the addition of either one of these to the other two would bring a bonus of more than a single hole.

I have also been working out the result of another golfing snare and delusion, which I confess to having worked to my advantage in earlier years in order to offset the result of some unfortunate speculations on the Turf. This is to challenge two or even three players—the better they are, the harder they fall—on the basis that you will play their best ball and their worst ball, receiving in the first instance the same start as you will concede in the second. In other words, if their best ball will give you four up, you will give their worst ball the same.

Those who wish to perpetrate this on non-readers of the *Sunday Times* (and serve them right!) should try to make the opening figure as high as possible—let us say four up. As argument proceeds and the victims start muttering in their corner, working out sums on their fingers, you distract their attention by making generous advances in the worst-ball odds, first to five up, and then, with piteous protests about daylight robbery, etcetera, to six. Daylight robbery indeed it is, but not on their part.

The scores of our quartet at Sunningdale (Old Course first) were: Clark 69, 70; Foster 74, 71; Tullis 72, 73; Bonallack 74, 72. What start could Clark have afforded to give the worst ball of these three not inconsiderable players? The answer is that he could have given them *eight up* on the Old and *twelve up* on the New and still have beaten them—and with that inside information I wish you the very best of luck with readers of the wrong paper next Sunday.

As to the matches at Limerick and the ability of three good amateurs to beat any professional, however distinguished, three low-handicap amateurs from Sunningdale did not share my doubts. What is more, they were supported by that expert calculator of the odds, Mr Tim Holland, of Crockfords. He would pay for the transportation of any professional, if I remember rightly, from America or elsewhere, if we would back him to play the three amateurs for £1,000. The *Sunday Times* duly searched its pockets—I fancy Lord Thomson was abroad at the time—but for one excellent reason or another the money did not seem to be quite forthcoming.

Judging by the results at Limerick, we appear to have been well out of it, since the professionals were beaten by three matches to one. Harry Weetman, deputizing for George Will, never got going and with scores of 76, 79 was beaten 11 and 9 and O'Connor (69, 74) by 8 and 6. David Thomas (75, 67) very nearly snatched a half, but the Irish international Ray Kane holed a fourteen-footer to beat him on the last green. The only winner, strangely enough, was Peter Alliss, who scored 68 and 66 and beat Jack Harrington, Rupert Staunton and Jimmy Bruen, who have played between them nineteen times for Ireland, by 3 and 2.

I say 'strangely enough', because when we found ourselves in Spain together recently Alliss said he had played a dozen such matches at weekends during the winter against members of his club, by no means as distinguished as the Irishmen, and won only two of them. In the middle of the series he holed Parkstone in 65 several times running and did not win once. He thought the pros were certain to lose. Ironically, he was the only one to win. Whether he would back himself every weekend to take on three internationals and hole an unseen course twice in 134 is another matter.

BLAST THAT BAKER!

Everything seemed to conspire this week to cause me to write about that variety of golf club known as the wedge. It is many a long year since I first heard the sage of American golf, Tommy Armour, pronounce this club to have been alone responsible for the lowering of championship scores since the thirties. His theory is echoed by Sam Snead in his book. 'This club is the principal reason why scoring generally has been lowered so fantastically since the Bobby Jones era, even though courses on the whole are longer and tougher.'

Snead himself is among its greatest exponents, and I retain the most vivid memory of him in a practice bunker before the Canada Cup at Buenos Aires. The bunker was completely flat and open, and the flag only a few yards on the green. He had tossed a dozen balls into the sand at random and proceeded to step from one to the other, splashing them nonchalantly out, several of them stone dead and the worst no more than five feet from the flag.

Gene Sarazen is generally accepted, both by himself and the others, as the inventor of the original wedge, or sand-iron. 'The wedge,' he writes in an American magazine, 'is a variation of the sand-iron I designed almost thirty-five years ago by adding solder to the back of a niblick. I was taking flying lessons at the time. I noticed when I pulled the stick the tail would lower and the plane would take off. It occurred to me that if I put a tail on a niblick I could get the ball up and out of the sand easier. I tried it and it worked.

'I didn't tell anyone about my discovery. I took the club with me to the British Open in 1932 and kept it hidden. When I showed during the first few holes that the club invariably could get me out of the sand and close enough to the hole to get down in one putt, everyone began talking about it. I won that championship by five strokes . . . and manufacturers started putting out sand-irons by the thousands.'

Nevertheless, it seems likely that the original sand-wedge was invented in 1928 by a Texas cotton-broker called Edwin Kerr McClaine, and this very club has been presented to the US Golf Association's museum in New York by Mrs Robert A. Benton, who came across it in the course of research for a biography of that great golfer, the late Horton Smith. In February 1930 Smith was playing at Houston, Texas, and was introduced to McClaine and to the 'freak niblick' with which he performed such remarkable feats.

The club had a hickory shaft, with a concave face and rounded sole, and had been made by a blacksmith. The average club weighs thirteen ounces. This one weighed twenty-three. Smith in an exhibition match on the following day played some impressive shots with it, and took

it along with him to Atlanta. From here he travelled with Bobby
Jones to the Savannah Open, sharing the same hotel suite, and one
may imagine the pair of them sitting up in the evenings, talking golf
and taking practice swings with Smith's new bludgeon. Nothing, of
course, would do but that Jones must have one too. The blacksmith
was summoned and in due course the twin was created.

And now, a few months later, the scene shifts to a lonely and
inwardly desperate figure standing behind the bunker on the left of
the 16th green at Hoylake. The figure is Jones and this is the fourth
round of the British Open, the year 1930. As he started this final
round, Archie Compston, 'hitting the ball like a frenzied giant', was
just finishing his third round in a record 68 to lead by one stroke.
'As he made his beaming way to the clubhouse through a myriad of
well-wishers,' Jones has recalled, 'he was about as happy a figure as
I have ever seen.'

Having hit one of the stewards on the head at the 2nd (is he still
around Hoylake today, I wonder?) and thereby achieving a fantastically lucky 3, Jones was just short of the 8th green in two, when out
of a blue sky there came, instead of a birdie 4, two fluffed chips, three
putts from ten feet—and a 7. He had taken 4 at each of the short
holes coming home and now, though he would have heard that
Compston was not doing well, he was not to know that the latter
was in fact piling up the 82 which left its mark on him for life. Jones
looks down at his ball. It is lying within a few inches of the very back
of the bunker.

'The slope of this back wall was quite abrupt . . . the ball could
only be struck by a sharply descending blow, and my right foot had
to be placed almost at the top of the bank behind me. The hole lay at
some 20 to 25 yards across this flat, shining green. I had not used for
an important shot during the whole year the massive, concave sand-
wedge which Horton Smith had given me earlier in the year. At St
Andrews I had hacked a ball out of a gorse bush with it . . . but as I
looked at this situation on the 70th hole of the championship I could
see that this was the only club with which this shot could be played
successfully. . . . I knew it was dangerous to use a club with which I
had so little familiarity, but it was the only hope. The shot came off
precisely as intended, the ball popped over the forward bank of the
bunker and crept slowly across the green until it just tickled the edge
of the hole and stopped two inches beyond. That did it.'

Thus did the long arm of chance reach out from the inventive
Texas cotton-broker to play its part in golfing history—for Jones's
victory was, of course, part of his famous 'Grand Slam'. This sort of
thing always fascinates me and I was about to pursue the theme—

rather interestingly, I thought—when I was interrupted only five minutes ago by the long arm of chance reaching out to me too, this time through a neighbour of mine, a retired civil servant of immense distinction and necessary anonymity, having thrown a dice onto the carpet some months ago.

As the dice fell, his wife marked little crosses on a football-pool coupon at appropriate intervals—and has been doing so each week ever since. On Saturday evenings she draws horizontal red lines and then looks vertically down the lines, or maybe vice versa—neither the distinguished civil servant nor I have the faintest comprehension what she is about—to see how many Xs there are in each line. Early this week she became strangely reticent. In one line there appeared to be seven. The eighth space was a blank, caused by the postponement of that great religious festival, Celtic *v.* Rangers. According to the Rules, she said, this counted as an away win, two points. There were only nine draws in all. We had seven of them—and the religious festival.*

For most of the week she has been cross-eyed from sitting up of a night counting and re-counting the Xs. All there. Had she posted the coupon? Surely, because an agent collected it and he gets two bob in the pound. Was her copy correct? Well, it always had been before. On Thursday, as the postman was still knocking, the child was waiting in the hall to collect the letters. 'Two for you, Mummy!' Trembling fingers. Two bills.

Now, however, all is well. It has come. £1,000. 17s. 0d. for one line and £38. 6s. 0d. for another, tossed in as though as an after-thought to buy drinks for a few of our friends. (Don't trouble. The party was last night.) Such is the well-merited reward of skill, initiative, leadership, enterprise, willingness to take risks in our Welfare State. And the beauty of it is that we only paid 5s. in tax on our £1,039. 3s. 0d., (one-quarter of our £1 stake), whereas if we had slaved away for a year writing a book or wasted our time flogging the export trade, we should have lost about £500—unless, of course, we proved very successful, in which case we should have lost a great deal more.

Yet how unkind, as the poet said, is the winter wind of man's ingratitude! Never mind our miserable £1,039. 3s. 0d. What about the baker who, out of the thousands of millions submitted, had the only winning line? £275,235! It's disgraceful. He ought to have been on strike. One turn of the dice on the carpet months ago, one more cross in the right place, and we should have had half of it.

* Thus described because one team is Catholic, the other Protestant. Such is the fervour engendered, and so violent are the rival Christians liable to become while watching the contest, that the Chief Constable of Glasgow would not permit it to be held on a Saturday.

£137,617. 10s. 0d. And my half would have been £68,808. 15s. 0d.
I see myself on the stage ('maximum publicity, please') accepting the
cheque from the budding film star; being interviewed, even, on the
telly. 'Will this make any difference to your life, Mr Longhurst?'
'Like hell it will—and my notice, as from Tuesday.' 'Mr Longhurst,
thank you.' 'Not at all, thank *you*!'*

* It is difficult indeed not to covet one's neighbour's goods, whatever the
Commandment may say. Huge advertisements by the pools firm on the following
Sunday showed the baker smiling genially, with the caption saying, 'He'll never
"*need*" dough again'! A newspaper interview said: 'His wife, Alice, still collects
trading stamps and cigarette coupons—she has set her heart on some cut glass
and a coffee table—and she continues to go to Bingo and whist.' Meanwhile an
accountant informs me that in order to *earn* the money which he won for a
penny (less one farthing tax) the baker would have to have an income of just
under £4,000,000 a year. Such is life! I am happy to report, however, that in a
survey of pools winners by *The Times* some time later Mr Wall, the baker, was
one of those to whom the money had brought happiness and contentment, not
only to himself but to his three children and sundry relatives, all of whom he
set up with the money.

BERKSHIRE 'BONKERS'

Despite their tendency to snivel, fidget, hiccough, and wander off looking for lark's nests, I have always had a soft spot for boy caddies. Carrying a golfer's clubs or, in these days of bags the size and weight of cabin trunks, pulling them round on a trolley, seems to me an ideal job for a boy, not merely because it is convenient for the increasingly portly golfers like myself, but because it gives the boys themselves an insight into adult life and may in many cases increase their vocabulary. Nor, one would have thought, is pocket money so abundant in the Affluent Society that anything from 10s. to 15s. is to be sneezed at in return for a four-mile walk. Alas, this happy source of fresh air, exercise, education and tax-free income is now, by an act of bureaucratic lunacy still difficult to credit, closed. The scene of the grotesque chain of events which caused this unfortunate situation was the Berkshire Club, where the accepted rate for boy caddies was 12s. 6d. per round if totally unskilled, 15s. if 'experienced'.

Having employed a boy who in his opinion fell only too clearly into the former category, a member handed him 12s. 6d. Not good enough, said the boy, and complained to his father, himself a regular Berkshire caddie. The member, politely refusing to budge, said that when the boy learned to keep up with the game and began to know what was going on, he, the member, would be only too delighted to reward him with 15s. The father thereupon informed the local authorities that the Berkshire Club were infringing the law by employing child labour.

At any rate, believe it or not, round came an official from the Education Department to the office of the club secretary, Mr J. W. Shaw, to challenge him with the dastardly offence of employing children, contrary to the Children and Young Persons Act, 1933 (as amended by the Education Act, 1944). Those who served in His Majesty's Army during the war, and doubtless other services too, will recognize this as a pass-the-buck situation if ever there was one and will salute Mr Shaw for his flawless handling of it. 'I am afraid I don't employ any caddies', he said.

The finger of guilt then pointed inexorably down the road to the caddie-master, who undoubtedly did employ caddies. The County of Berks booklet on bye-laws relating to the Employment of Children and Street Trading, a copy of which I have before me, was brandished before him; the caddie-master, we may assume, scratched an incredulous head, as I have been doing; and the net result was that there have been no boy caddies at the Berkshire ever since.

I have been studying the booklet with an awful fascination. It is an

emblem of that shadowy Other World, which the rest of us fear
because we cannot comprehend. One can think, for instance, of a
hundred occupations in which it would seem proper to prohibit the
employment of children. The booklet, however, lists ten. How many,
I wonder, can you guess? Incidentally a 'child' is anyone within the
compulsory school age of fifteen, though 'for the purposes of this
Note, a child attains a given age on the day previous to his birthday'.
Make it 14 years 364 days, then—except of course in leap years.

I am sorry to inform those of our readers who follow the honourable
calling of hairdresser that the first—I will not say worst—prohibited
employment is that of 'lather boy to a barber or hairdresser'. Don't
ask me why! Others, I will not quote them all, are 'in the kitchen of a
fried-fish shop; as marker in a billiard or bagatelle saloon; in connection
with the sale of intoxicating liquor "except when such liquors are
sold exclusively in sealed containers"; in selling theatre programmes;
in collecting or sorting rags or refuse; or in connection with race-
courses or slaughter-houses'.

No child under thirteen is allowed to earn pocket money at anything
but an exception in Para. 3 seemed to offer a gleam of light when I
noted the words 'light agricultural or horticultural work'. This
seemed as good a definition of golf as I had read for some time, but
unfortunately the employer may only be the parent or guardian.

A boy may not earn money on Sundays except between 8 a.m.
and 10 a.m., which I am afraid would not find the average member
of the Berkshire to have progressed very far from the clubhouse
before the boy had to down tools and walk in, but another ray of
hope seemed to shine out from Para. 6, which declares that a child
may be employed for five hours between 7 a.m. and 7 p.m. on a
Saturday, or other school holidays, provided (a) that he also has
five hours' continuous rest, and (b) that the employer sees that he is
suitably shod and suitably clad for protection against the weather.

As usual however 'they' win in the end—with a knock-out in the
shape of Para. 9, sub-sections (a) to (f), which I wish I had space to
quote in full. It is true that we can employ a boy caddie on a Saturday
or other school holiday for five hours at a time, which should get us
round eighteen holes in this country, if not in America, but—wait for
it!—the employer (and I can see a nice argument between the caddie-
master and the golfer as to which is the employer. 'Not me sir. No,
sir. You, sir!'), the employer shall within four days 'send a written
notification to the local authority stating his name and address, the
name, address, and date of birth of the child, the occupation in which
and the place at which, the child is employed, and the times at which
the employment begins and ends'.

When this is done, the local authority will issue the child with a card, hereinafter called an 'Employment Card', and no child shall be employed unless he has it with him. Furthermore, within fourteen days there shall be produced to (presumably by the child) and endorsed by the golfer—or the reluctant caddie-master, whichever emerges as the employer—'a certificate (for which no charge shall be made) from the School Medical Officer that the health and physical development of the child are such that the employment will not render him unfit to obtain proper benefit from his education'.

Nor is this all. The employer—I think this one really must be passed to the caddie-master!—'shall keep affixed in a conspicuous position in the place in, or in connection with which, the child is employed, a notice showing the name, address and date of birth of the child, the occupation in which, and the times within which, the child may be employed on school days, on Sundays, and on weekdays when school is not open'.

When you consider that a 'child' may be a whacking great youth of six feet, weighing twelve stone and capable of tearing public telephones apart with his bare hands, it seems bureaucracy run riot to protect him with all this rigmarole from the sweated labour of earning 15s. by voluntarily pulling a bag of clubs round a golf course. Does this sort of bye-law apply all over the country, I wonder, and are all of us who delight in seeing a boy earn in this way pocket money on a scale we never enjoyed ourselves villains of the deepest dye? Or is it only Berkshire that's bonkers?

OLD KNICKER-MAN IN THE WOODS

I must confess that I think *Golf Illustrated*'s South African correspondent, Ronald Norval, has probably done a service not only to the game but in the end to the objects of his criticism, in writing, obviously more in sorrow than in anger, that some of the younger British professionals at the moment touring South Africa 'look a very sloppy bunch' by comparison with their local counterparts. 'Not only were some of their hats of the kind that father reserves for gardening', he added, 'but their slacks were creased and at least one played with his shirt outside his trousers. This sort of thing does little to help the image of professional golf.'

I remember distinctly reading only recently—it may have been in something by Horace Hutchinson, who won the first two Amateur Championships in 1886 and 1887 but continued as a great figure long after that—how it was the fashion, particularly in Scotland, where, after all, the most 'fashionable' golf was played, to wear one's oldest and most dilapidated clothes for golf, and how they used almost to rival each other in the raggedness of the coats in which they played. Anyone who turned up for golf smartly turned out automatically proclaimed himself a bounder.

To play without a coat at all, however, was equally out of line, and in 1901 the editor of *Golf Illustrated* in a powerful editorial wrote: 'I devoutly hope that the American custom of playing golf in shirtsleeves will never obtain in this country. If the weather is too hot for a flannel jacket, it is too hot for golf.'

When I first became conscious of golf, in the twenties, everyone played in a coat or blazer. I remember seeing Mitchell and Duncan play and they wore coats and plus-fours. Does anyone old enough to remember them, and Harry Vardon, recall ever having seen them play in trousers, I wonder? The very idea of Abe Mitchell in trousers seems as 'foreign' as would have been that of Archie Compston in plus-fours.

I suppose I began to become clothes-conscious on the links in the late twenties and early thirties, and on the whole this was sartorially a pretty ghastly period. The combination of a Fair Isle pullover, plus-fours almost down to the ankles (often grey flannel at that), and 'co-respondent' shoes of brown and white or, even nattier, black and white, is not one in which I should care to see printed a photograph of myself today. 'Natty', however, was the word according to our lights at the time.

I have not the slightest doubt that the idea of the well-dressed golfer emanated from America, more perhaps in the person of Walter

Hagen than anyone. Hagen was always flawlessly turned out and would often change his attire between one round and the next on the same day. He was flamboyant perhaps by British standards, but this depends—I don't know whether you have ever thought of it—on light. I only realized this when I went to the 1955 Ryder Cup match at the Thunderbird Club in the desert in California, where the atmosphere is crystal clear and the sun shines all day long. People there look perfectly normal and excite no comment in rigouts so bizarre and grotesque as would bring gales of laughter if sported by a music-hall comedian in Britain. Their cars are painted in at least two bright colours and one soon realizes that a shiny black Rolls-Royce, which looks the height of elegance when sweeping up the Mall, would look more like a hearse in the vivid light of the desert. My esteemed colleague Leonard Crawley, resplendent in an all-red suit, looked exactly right!

If the clothing worn by Hagen and some of his fellow Americans like Johnny Farrell, who was always being voted the 'best-dressed golfer'—I forget by whom—seemed a little flamboyant by our standards, it should be remembered that it was not so by theirs.

I suppose it was the war that set us back to the comparative soberness of attire that is fashionable today. Practically no one wears plus-fours, and the more's the pity. David Blair turned out in a splendid white pair, topped off with a Panama hat with regimental ribbon, for the Walker Cup match at Portland, Oregon, and when he drove into the trees drew from a spectator the immortal observation, 'I guess the old knicker-man is in the woods.' None of the current millionaire golfers, however, wear anything but trousers, and generally sober-hued at that. Anything else would nowadays be regarded as something of a gimmick.

In the United States, Jimmy Demaret took as his 'signature tune', so to speak, the wearing of bizarre colours, even by the sunniest standards, and over here Max Faulkner has done the same. I trust that I shall not be held to be being personal if I say that Faulkner, even if his colours are on the bright side for our dull climate, is always most impeccably turned out and in this respect is a model for all to follow. Professional golfers nowadays, in so far as they are tournament players, are entertainers and in the public limelight—unlike, in case anyone is unkind enough to point out that I am not myself the best-dressed character at the Open Championship, golf writers.

As a journalist, one is always, or should be, an observer rather than a participator, and in this capacity, I confess that I find it strange that in a beautiful setting like Gleneagles professionals should come into the dining-room for breakfast and lunch not only without a coat, but without even a tie. Yet how unjust is this comment, for I am thinking mainly of the professional-amateur tournament, and it is the amateurs surely who should set the example—and many of them have no coats or ties in the dining-room either.

THIRTY YEARS TOO SOON

'If only I had been playing today I should have been a millionaire.' Such were the wistful words of Cary Middlecoff during the Carling Tournament outside Boston a few months ago, the winner of which—Tony Lema, as it turned out—was due to receive the equivalent of some £12,500 in our money. Middlecoff, though dreadfully slow, was a very great player. He won the US Open twice, the Masters once. The only trouble was that he did it just a tantalizingly few years too soon.

Last year Jack Nicklaus created a huge sensation during the Masters by holing the Augusta National course in 64. People forgot that Middlecoff had done it too—ten years before. Even as late as 1961, when Gary Player won the Masters, his manager, Mark McCormack, assured me that he had so arranged his affairs that in the fullness of time his victory would secure him not less than a million dollars.

If Middlecoff was too early by ten years, Alfred Padgham, who died last week, was too early by thirty. One wonders what, in today's terms, he would have won in his 'golden year' of 1936. There were not, of course, so many tournaments then, but I seem to remember that he won every one of them except one—having already in the previous autumn won the Match-Play Championship. Certainly he won the first three—at Bramshot (surely the greatest single golfing casualty of the war), Moor Park and Southport—and soon it was time to report for the Open at Hoylake.

Never had such a test been presented to the experts. New tees had stretched the course to 7,078 yards, with immense 'carries', and the rough was like hay. 'If the wind blows,' said some of the prophets, hoping, as always, that it would, 'four 80s may be good enough.' Some of the lesser fry declared the course 'impossible'. Padgham sailed round in his first practice round in 68, reaching every green in two. 'Padgham Expected To Win', said the *Sunday Times* headline, I am happy to see, the day before the championship.

One of Padgham's greatest assets was his absolute imperturbability. He spoke slowly and quietly, moving neither head nor hands to make his point, and took in his stride everything that came his way. It was a quality which was to stand him in good stead at Hoylake.

On the final day Padgham, with four others, was one stroke behind Bill Cox and James Adams and was drawn early. He arrived to find the pro's shop, in which he had left his clubs, bolted and barred. In the scene which ensued he remained the least moved. With four minutes to go he instructed his caddie—who is still a regular at professional tournaments today—to smash the window and break into the shop. How many, I wonder, either then or today, could have walked as placidly to the tee and, without a single practice shot, gone round in 71?

In the afternoon, with Adams half an hour behind but still one shot ahead, Padgham did the first four holes on the way home in 13. Adams countered with a 3 and a 2 at the 10th and 11th. At last a tremendous cheer told the luckless Adams that his rival had holed for a 3 at the 18th—with a putt of a good five yards—and eventually he too needed a 3 to tie. His ball actually touched the hole, swung round and stayed agonizingly out.

The first qualifying day was washed out by a thunderstorm, which among other things rendered void a record 67 by Cotton at Wallasey and knocked a reporter unconscious by telephone at Hoylake. On a humbler level I myself had to fill out a long-drawn ten minutes on the BBC's Empire service about the golf that never was, but this was much enlivened by a waitress with a huge pile of plates tripping over a guy-rope just outside our little box and going down with a crash that reverberated throughout the Empire.

I mention these details because it seems to indicate the fairness of the more modern systems of 'leaders out last' in place of chancing the luck of the draw. Some may say that they would prefer to 'know what they had to do', as Adams did. For myself I would rather, like Padgham, get my blow in first and let the other man sweat it out for the next half-hour trying to equal it.

Another of Padgham's assets was a huge pair of hands, with strength to match. A friend of mine swore blind that he had once been playing with Padgham at Knowle Park when they had noticed three of the green-keeping staff trying unsuccessfully to shift a small tree trunk. Padgham asked them where they were trying to put it—and then put it there.

Despite his strength he was the complete classical stylist at golf, with an unhurried, rhythmic swing that was a joy to watch. Furthermore, he simplified golf in a way which could have a strong appeal to any club golfer today. He was, as he called it, a 'one-shot man'. In other words, he 'felt' the same shot with every club in the bag. He would position the ball differently of course, and take a fuller or shorter swing according to the distance, but basically they were all the same shot.

From this, one day, came the turning-point. He noticed that he was far more liable to lay chip shots within inches of the hole, or even to hole them, than long putts. Why, it occurred to him, should putting be different, a game within a game? Why should it not be merely the shortest version of his 'one shot'? He tried it, hanging his

left arm down straight in line with the club instead of cocking the
elbow and ensuring that his eye was directly over the ball. The result
was sensational. In tournament after tournament he holed putt after
putt and this, with his beautiful long game, made him for a year
unbeatable.

In an effort to 'cash in' on the Open he was persuaded to tour
South Africa, but, alas, the nap on the greens not only defeated him
but destroyed his touch and the war virtually put paid to his career
as a tournament golfer. He became a war-reserve policeman, and with
his huge hands and feet, his slow way of speaking, his height and his
absolute 'unflappability' one can think of no better man for the job.

I see that after the Open I advised him in print 'not to accept a penny
less than fifty guineas' for exhibition matches. And nowadays Arnold
Palmer plays twenty-five a year, almost as a sideline, at £1,375 apiece
—quite apart, of course, from all the advance publicity which is
handled—whoever would have guessed?—by Arnold Palmer Printing
Inc.! All of which only goes to show it is not so much what you do:
it's also when you do it.

H

BEWARE THE MARTINIS!

A 'completely obsessed' golfer of twenty-three informs me that he has had the good fortune to secure a job in Denver, Colorado— 'incidentally at a ridiculously high salary and I cannot understand why more people of my age are not hot-footing it out there'—and asks if I will reveal to him 'just what this game of golf is in America'. Since American golf and golfers are so constantly in the news, and will be especially so when that notable pair, Nicklaus and Palmer, arrive here in a week or two for the Open, I thought I would try to answer our enviable reader's question here.

He will find golf in America, I suspect, an almost completely different game, some aspects of which he will like, others perhaps not. The first difference, from which stem many of the others, is that the Americans are, and always have been since the very beginnings of golf in their country, of the opinion that golf is basically a stroke-play, rather than a match-play, game. This is a wholly logical approach. They set out to play eighteen holes of golf and eighteen holes they are jolly well going to play.

Their primary object is to see how many they can go round in, or 'shoot'. They are not interested in picking up their ball, as we do, because their partner has won the hole for their side. Indeed, I have played in four-balls where no sides were picked at all; we simply played round, each of us, or at any rate three of the party, recording all the scores at each hole—including, to my great mortification, my own. Mostly, however, they will make up some sort of match, but it is still their own score that they are thinking of—and the scores of perhaps a dozen others with whom they have made all sorts of complicated wagers, to be worked out later over drinks in the locker-room.

This, of course, leads to the second, much-publicized difference, against whose influence we are fighting a none too successful rear-guard action over here, namely slow play. 'Golf is not a funeral,' Bernard Darwin once wrote, 'though both can be very sad affairs.' Four-ball stroke-play, with four indifferent club players holing out at every hole, is bound to be funereal, and the first thing our young friend will have to do is to learn to live with it. When after about three hours the usual messages begin to come up regarding the anticipated pint of beer at the 19th, he will have to send back the disquieting intelligence that they are only sitting on the 11th tee and there remain at least another two hours to go. Also that it is no good his stomach talking about pints of beer: all it is going to get is a rather weak form of lager, so cold as to freeze its very lining.

As to the golf itself, it is possible to portray a typical course more truly than could be done in this country. The picture is of a park-like country-club course, quite hilly, tree-lined, cut perhaps out of the vast acreage of scrub and forest which took possession of the land when the original settlers just abandoned it and moved west. The greens will be bigger than here, with separate 'pin-positions', and a straight putt will be a rarity. Though spectacular advances have been made by the 'agronomists' in adapting grasses to the varying climates in the United States, the newcomer will find that on the whole the grass is coarser-bladed than here and, through heavy watering, more lush. The run-up approach will soon be but a memory.

The odds are that he will find himself playing at a golf- and country-club combined, for which the subscription will be anything from treble to ten times what we pay in England. A comparatively modest country club, however, will have a pool, and a magnificent locker-room, according to our undemanding and insanitary standards, complete with attendants, possibly a masseur, showers and, what even we might soon aspire to, something to put on your hair afterwards. There will be a beautiful drawing-room, scarcely used except for formal occasions, a card-room, and that most insidious of institutions, the men's grill.

I say 'insidious' because the men's grill is open all day and is therefore one of the main causes of slow play among club golfers. It does not matter when they finish. Bar service (Beware the Martinis, my young friend. Always look on the bottle and when it says '100 proof' have a care!), steaks, huge ribs of roast beef, three-decker sandwiches, the lot—are all perpetually 'on'. So if they take five hours, well, they have come out for a day's golf anyway and have had more of it than if they had gone round in four. All the same, we should not hear so much about slow play in America if lunch were 'off' on the dot of half-past two!

The pro's shop will be reminiscent of one of our better sports-goods stores and the pro himself, as here, an excellent and respected citizen. There will be no secretary, but instead a highly paid club manager, for this is no small business. With everybody signing chits for everything, even the caddie's tip—and after the first two 100-proof Martinis signing blithely and with no pain at all—the turnover is liable to be very considerable.

This, I hope my American friends would agree, is a fair picture of a typical country club, lavish perhaps by comparison with our own, but then it is the playground not only of the golfer but of the family. There are, of course, extremes above and below. Many a public-course golfer, in order to be sure of a Sunday game, queues up at midnight on Saturday, but, if he does secure a starting time, he is at least sure of a day's golf. His round may take him seven hours.

At the other end of the scale one could quote the late George S. May's Tam O'Shanter club outside Chicago which, in his day at any rate, had eleven bars, a telephone on every tee, and a special 'quiet room' where people could retreat from the otherwise incessant piped-in music. Or a Californian club where a week-end's compulsory hire not only of an electric buggy but also a caddy to hold the flag costs more than a year's golf at most clubs over here and a local rule declares that 'a player on foot has no standing on the course'.

It takes all sorts to make the world of golf. My prophecy is that our young friend will thoroughly enjoy his golf in America and the warm-hearted welcome that will assuredly go with it. His salary, he says, is ridiculously high—and so, for that matter, is Denver, Colorado. The city, we may assume, will remain at its present altitude. Whether the salary will appear so elevated after a few months of golf is another matter.

NOTHING TO BEAT THE REAL THING

'Of all the phenomena connected with the rise and fall of British pastimes, none is so remarkable as the progress of golf—an advance so recent and yet so powerful as to sweep away comparison in any other field. Statistics are eloquent of the giant strides taken by the Royal and Ancient game.'

I seem to have read this somewhere before. Indeed, I seem more than once to have written about this golfing 'explosion', as it is now called, myself, but, alas, the more you write about golf the more you realize that it has all been said before, for the passage I have quoted comes, believe it or not, from the *Strand Magazine* of May 1906. My eye lit upon it as I was thumbing through my much-prized bound copies, looking for the original illustrations of Mr Josiah Amberley in 'The Retired Colourman' to compare them with the recent episode in the BBC's Sherlock Holmes series.

Three maps of the British Isles, with each golf club represented by a dot, show the state of affairs in 1886, 1896, and 1906. The first is comparatively bare, with a peppering of clubs round Edinburgh and in Fife, though very few round Glasgow: only forty in England, and three in Ireland—one at Dublin, one somewhat south-west and the third somewhere near Cork, though which these were I do not know.

Twenty years later there were 500 clubs in all. The 'Emerald Isle', in the jargon of the day, has risen from 3 to 130 and the 'Land of the Leek' ('which has reared the football heroes of the past season') has replaced the virgin blankness of 1886 with 15 dots. Even the Isle of Man now has 3. As to the players, says the writer, Mr A. Wallis Myers (any relation, one wonders, to the present correspondent of the *Atlanta Journal*, whom we meet at the Masters each year?), they have increased thirty times—'an eloquent testimony to the generative powers of the pastime'.

Wandering through the *Strand*'s world of sixty years ago—*Puck of Pook's Hill* is just beginning in serial form, while Conan Doyle's *Sir Nigel* is on Chapter IV—I cannot resist the temptation of quoting an aside, unrelated to my supposed subject, portraying Colonel the Right Hon. Mark Lockwood defending, as does Mrs Bessie Braddock today, his stewardship as chairman of the Kitchen Committee.

'Even the House of Commons,' he says, 'includes among its members some who desire to secure the maximum of satiety with the minimum of expenditure,' and he does not see what they have got to complain about when they can get a solid three-course lunch, including choice of two hot joints and two veg, for one shilling.

What is more, declares the Colonel, the committee has been able to reduce the excellent Cliquot '93 from 10s. a bottle to 8s. 6d., the St Julien '93 from 3s. to 2s., while 'an exceedingly cheap and genuine claret may be purchased for tenpence a bottle'.

They also, incidentally, maintain a 708-gallon vat of constantly maturing ten-year-old whisky, never permitted to fall below 350 gallons. No wonder they called it the best club in London!

Returning to my theme, a 1906 title 'The Funniest Golf Story' naturally catches the eye. Illustrious figures send in their contributions and here at last must surely be found some lively additions to the repertoire of the hard-pressed after-dinner speakers of today. Alas, we are back, so far as the golfing raconteur is concerned, to original sin.

James Braid sends in the one about the man clearing the 'bonnie wee burn' in the morning and going into 'that miserable sewer' in the afternoon. Harry Rountree, one of the greatest artists of the day, contributes at considerable length the one about the Indian Army colonel in a bunker dashing his club against a rock and saying, 'It's better to break one's clubs than lose one's temper.' Andrew Lang tells one 'which has already delighted more than one generation of golfers' —good heavens, how old can this one be?

It turns out to be the one about the golfer who descended into the sandpit, periodically hacking up clouds of sand, and on emerging was asked how many he had played. The punch line is: 'I went into that place at a quarter past twelve. It is now quarter to one. You are at liberty, sir, to form your own estimate.'

Artists also contribute their 'best', of which Starr Wood's may be taken to be quite a superior example. 'Confound it, sir, you nearly hit my wife.' 'Did I, sir? Well, you have a shot at mine.' Oh dear, oh dear!

Sometimes, however, connections with the present quicken the interest. Where, for instance, was, or is, the ladies' course at Deal, on which Will Owen was playing with W. W. Jacobs (both currently appearing in the *Strand*), when Jacobs said to his young caddy, 'Do you get many people playing here?' and the boy (at least two of whose grandsons I suspect to have caddied for me in the Halford-Hewitt) replied, 'No, sir—only ladies and old gentlemen wot can't play.'

And was Westward Ho!—does anyone remember?—the West of England course where Braid and other eminent professionals were playing when, he relates, some trainers appeared, galloping their horses across the links. To induce them to take an interest in the game and spare the links they were invited to watch. After a while, says Braid, one of them said, 'Well, after seeing some of you play your approach strokes and the divots you remove, what puzzles me is why you should complain about the damage done by our horses!'

On the whole, I am afraid, it all seems to prove, as I have long suspected, that the best of 'made-up' golf stories were not, are not, and never really will be as funny as the real thing. The undergraduate, for instance, hurling his putter from the 5th green at Mildenhall and then having to wade in and recover it from two feet of icy water . . . my distinguished professional partner in the Bowmaker tournament at Sunningdale heaving his club into the wood at the 16th and finding it unretrievable up a tree . . . three of us standing in absolute silence on the 1st at Hoylake as our friend, A.T., prepares to play his third shot—four minds with but a single thought. 'No power on earth can prevent it. He is going to socket it at right-angles, out of bounds and into the Field.' Click—and the deed was done.

I suppose it was a shame to laugh, but, as the undergraduate said to the magistrate, 'I can only say, sir, that it appeared to be very funny at the time.'

NO BOASTING AT ST ANDREWS

A casual reference to the great Horace Hutchinson's having written in the original Badminton volume on golf that, on account of the excellence of the greens, more long putts were 'held' at Hoylake than elsewhere has given rise to a gratifying amount of curiosity and comment. For myself, having so often heard the expression, especially among professionals, I had imagined 'held' instead of 'holed' to be merely a survival of a slipshod expression which by the nineties had become such common currency that even so un-slipshod a writer as Hutchinson accepted it.

The main school of thought, however, headed by that master wordsman Stephen Potter, maintains that he meant that the greens have been so good, more putts were held on their line at Hoylake— the suggestion that more putts were holed there being patently absurd, as another correspondent points out, since this would depend on the number of people playing.

As against that, a 'lifelong teacher of English' and ex-resident of Hoylake says he will be delighted to confuse me further by referring me to the second slip who held a miraculous catch, the tennis player who held his service, the rugger club which held its annual dance and England who never held their heavier opponents.

The central idea is that 'something was carried through to a successful conclusion' and in this sense the player held his putt as well as holed it. 'Why holed out?' says another letter. 'It ought to be holed in'—but we will leave that.

Another suggestion is that the expression derives from the earlier incident when a Hoylake golfer's ball was undoubtedly 'held' by the hole, this time a rabbit-hole. He could see it but could not extract it and was about to drop another over his shoulder when his opponent claimed the hole—the rule then being, of course, 'lost ball, lost hole'. The committee upheld the opponent whereupon the player stalked out of the club, declaring that he would never darken the links again till he had trained a ferret.

The idea also seems common that, just as the hole is often said to 'gobble up' putts, it is only natural that it should normally be taken to hold them, the correct expression therefore being that the putts were held. Much simpler is the explanation of another reader who dismisses the whole thing as a misprint. The compositor set up 'hold' instead of 'holed', whereupon the alert proof-reader, noting a wrong tense, altered it to 'held'.

Alas for such simplicity. Another diligent student of Hutchinson's works finds in his *Golfing*, dated 1893, the same year as my original quotation: 'His brother Andrew [Kirkcaldy] is only one behind him, having recently held out in 74.'

As I contemplate this innocent but controversial four-letter word, a vague sense of distate begins to come over me. Then suddenly it is a perishing February morning and I am back on the barrack square of the aptly named Saighton camp near Chester—can it really be twenty-five years ago?—being initiated into the mysteries of the Bofors gun. Whatever the order might be, the drill began with: 'No. 4 will ensure that the lever foot-pedal held is at foot-pedal held and report "held".' One always seemed to be No. 4. We might not know how the damned things went into the auto-loader or how to put the breech-block together, but we were always safe in shouting 'held'. We almost did it in our sleep. I now cast it from my mind for ever and the correspondence is hereby closed.

Arising out of it, however, is a story, new to me, of the great Hoylake hero, John Ball, which some members of the Royal Liverpool club may be able to confirm, or otherwise. Ball, it is said, sent his clubs by rail to Westward Ho! for the championship of 1912 and proceeded there himself on an old boneshaker motor-bicycle—which must have been no mean ride from Hoylake. The clubs were lost on the railway—'twas ever thus—so he picked out a selection from the pro's shop, and duly won the championship. This was the year he beat Abe Mitchell, then an artisan amateur, at the 38th in the final.

I do not, I trust, live in the past, but the early days of golf have always intrigued me and I am indebted to a kindly correspondent from Kent for the loan of an 1837 edition of Dr Grierson's *Delineations of St Andrews*, whose last chapter is entitled 'Company of Golfers'.

I think it was Eric Brown who referred to the Old Course as a 'dirt track', but he was not being quite so rude as people thought, for the doctor also referred to it as a track, though admittedly omitting the dirt. The holes, he says, are mostly a quarter of a mile long and the links (in the plural) are 'perhaps superior to any in the kingdom'.

What surprises me is his description of the play. One had thought golf to be a case of match-play or stroke-play, the former more highly thought of in this country, the latter in America, but at St Andrews in those early days it seems to have been a question of, so to speak, 'hole-play'. You could play as many of the holes as you liked, says the doctor, but play may be said to terminate at each of them.

You counted your strokes, it seemed, not as a total for the hole but only in relation to the other side. If you were level, the next man played 'the odds'—today we should call it 'the odd'—and then, if necessary, the 'two more', the 'three more', and so on, while the other side in due course played 'one off three', etcetera. You just went on till one side got its ball into the hole.

A minimum set of clubs was four—the play club, the spoon, the putter and the iron—but most golfers carried ten or a dozen. Good players, it also surprises me to learn, could hit a 'feathery' ball 180 to 200 yards.

Six men were employed in making the balls at a rate of nine a day each, and apart from the local consumption of 300 dozen they 'exported' over 8,500 a year to such places as Edinburgh, Glasgow, Aberdeen and Perth. Many of the ball-makers, it is observed, 'fall sacrifices to consumption; whether it be that the flue arising from the musty feathers they use being inhaled by the breath communicates a taint to lungs, or that the mode of forcing in these feathers confines and injures the chest'.

'Our late lamented King, William the Fourth' had recently presented to the Royal and A. the gold medal which is now played for at the Autumn Meeting and I commend to the present holder and future winners, and indeed to all club champions, the splendid custom which prevailed in 1837 and should never surely have been allowed to die out.

'The winner is obliged to wear his medal at all golf meetings at St Andrews, and *no other golfer, in the presence of the medallist, can be allowed to boast of his play or the superiority of his prowess on the links.*'

GOLFERS ON SERIOUS CHARGE

An enterprising magazine, *Golf World*, has been holding a kind of mass observation in miniature to determine what I believe is called in the jargon of the day the 'behaviour pattern' of the keen golfer. This is not to be confused with that more commonplace, though indispensable, human unit, the Average Golfer. The specimens observed had to be keen enough first of all to be among those 5,000 actual subscribers to the magazine to whom a long and detailed questionnaire was sent, and then to be among the 1,626 keen enough to answer it. The results, the magazine claims, may be assumed to relate to golfers as a whole, but this I take leave to doubt. Not all of us are such keen types as all that. All the same, some of the results do surprise me.

Until the fatal day when, with the best will in the world, the authorities on both sides of the Atlantic agreed to limit the number of clubs to fourteen, thus almost overnight condemning vast numbers of golfers, in order to keep up with the Joneses, to carry that number instead of the seven or eight which had previously sufficed (or to pull them round in a perambulator), it would have been useless to ask people how long they had their clubs, for they would have replied, 'Which ones?' Those were the days when you picked them up, one or two at a time, as they happened to take your fancy.

Now that they come in 'sets' the results are illuminating. Of the 1,609 who answered the particular question no fewer than 43 per cent have had their clubs for only two years or less. Does this reflect, I wonder, the tremendous upsurge of the game in recent years, the golfing 'explosion' as it is called, or is it that the affluent society enables people to emulate so many American golfers who, for prestige purposes, change their clubs every year, as they do their cars, just when they are nicely 'run in'?

Only one-fifth have had their clubs for five years or more, but at the far end of the scale we have the truly faithful veterans—two of whom have had the same clubs for forty years, one for forty-five, one for forty-six, and one (who is he and can we please hear more about him and his clubs in the next issue?)—for the full half-century.

Almost a third, it was found, belonged to more than one club. Can this, the compilers ask, be one reason for long waiting-lists at so many clubs? I suppose it might, but the true capacity of a club is limited, surely, by the number of members who want to play at the same time and a man cannot be on more than one course at once. There can be few more desirable members from the club treasurer's point of view than the fellow who has paid his subscription and is playing somewhere else.

I was surprised to find that 86 per cent of these enthusiasts play in club events and even more so that 68 per cent go and watch golf tournaments. When you consider how much better you can see it on the telly, here is dedication indeed. Still, there is no substitute really for being able to come home and say, 'I was there'—which is why, as I trust Mrs Castle is aware, people take their cars on to the Exeter by-pass on a Bank Holiday, knowing perfectly well they are going to be stationary for seven hours.

I am sometimes taken to task by eminent golfing legislators for paying too much attention to professional golf and too little to amateur. In defence, I usually reply that, while in my opinion little would be lost to the game itself if no professional tournaments were ever played again and that the whole justification of golf is the happiness it gives to the rank and file who play it, however indifferently they may do so, still, people in the main prefer to read about the great players, whether they be the current experts, who are million-aires, or Walter Hagen, who merely lived like one.

The question asked was in fact: 'Do you prefer to watch top-class amateur or professional tournaments?'—not: 'Do you prefer to read about them.' The answers, however, seem so conclusive that they must cover both. Allowing for some who did not reply, 88 per cent would watch professional golf against 6 per cent for amateur. The truth is, of course, that the man the golfer is really interested in is himself. If I could come up with something guaranteed to put twenty yards on the club golfer's drive, he would not give Palmer or Nicklaus a second thought.

Smoking and golf seem always to have gone together. Many of the game's greatest figures have been chain-smokers on the links. Others preferred a pipe. One hears of Harry Vardon sitting placidly on the tee box, smoking his pipe and waiting for the crowds to be cleared away, while those two mighty hitters, Ted Ray and Cyril Tolley, actually played with pipes in their mouths, though I can never quite see how.

Arnold Palmer gave up cigarettes for a while but nearly went round the bend and had to start again. Yet the answer to the question about smoking was: Yes, 51 per cent; No, 49 per cent.

The most astonishing result, however, is left to the end. Whatever may be said about golfers, they must, of all players of games, be by common consent the most abstemious. Yet the survey purports to show that, while 1,422 'indulge', only 195 do not. Such experience as I have had of golf and golfers convinces me that this serious charge is due to a misprint and that the two figures must somehow have become reversed.

CHIPERS, SMUDGERS AND JIGGERS

In the questionnaire which I was last mentioning a golfer admitted to having been playing with the same clubs for fifty years. It seemed to be a long time, but apparently this is not so. One correspondent, of many, says he purchased his putter—for half-a-crown—sixty-five years ago, his mashie sixty and his niblick fifty. 'The remainder,' he adds, 'are all new, having been acquired at odd times within the last fifteen or twenty years from money received from the Insurance Company.' Here is an intriguing thought, though I trust it will not put ideas into the heads of our younger and less pecunious readers. The idea of buying a job lot of ancient hickory clubs and replacing them with the modern article one by one at the expense of members of Lloyd's Golf Club is not without its attraction.

My own relations with the golfing insurance world remain cordial, but will not, I am afraid, have labelled me as a model client. In the days when I was actually invited to play in exhibition matches (interval for incredulous laughter) I struck a spectator on the head with a high slice—we remain friends to this day—as a result of which he not only went to hospital but also sold me a golfer's insurance policy. Within a week I had broken a steel-shafted two-iron and recovered twice the amount of the premium.

Later I decided to add an expensive shooting-stick to the policy and an extra premium of half-a-crown was duly negotiated. A few days later I left the stick in the electric train on returning to Liverpool from the Open Championship at Southport, and my claim for £12.10s. crossed in the post with the insurer's receipt for the half-crown. They suggested that perhaps 'in view of the circumstances, it would do if they only paid half', but I stood firm.

I recalled for them the case of the well-known London golfer playing a young fellow in a Continental championship. Having driven into the rough, he first tried his brassie behind the ball but eventually worked his way down and played out with his niblick. His opponent having cleared his throat rather suggestively, our friend replied, 'Look here, son. If I am going to cheat I start with the niblick and work up to the brassie.'

I often think that what one might call 'modern' golf—that is, the sort of game which may validly be compared with today's—started after the First World War, though I should not be surprised if senior observers better qualified to express an opinion assured me that the great triumvirate of Vardon, Taylor and Braid, despite the methods illustrated and described in their books, played the game in its 'modern' version.

One thing is certain, namely that for all the talk about 'craftsmen' the clubs used not only by Vardon and his contemporaries but even by Jones and Hagen, right up to the very late twenties, made the game more difficult, and a more delicate work of art, than it is today.

Two of these clubs come to mind. I have often, for instance, taken out of its case at the Royal and Ancient the driver which Vardon won his last Open in 1914—incidentally one of the eight clubs he carried on that occasion. It is, I suppose, a 'modern' club, certainly beautifully made, but one feels somehow that, even in its original condition, a couple of bashes by Nicklaus must have broken it in half.

Again, the 'mashie-iron' with which Bobby Jones played his immortal shot from the bunker at the 17th to win the 1926 Open at Lytham hung for many years in the clubhouse for anyone to take down and waggle. (Ethical standards in Lancashire being presumably not what they used to be, the club is now nailed to the wall!) At any rate it seems impossible with its thin grip, its thin, delicate shaft and lightweight head to think of hitting a ball 170 yards from a bunker. If Jones could do that with that, what could he not have done with the supremely effective clubs they make today—and none better, if I may strike a commercially patriotic note, than some of those made in this country.

I am sorry, of course, that, apart from driver and putter, the old names have disappeared and we no longer get those maids-of-all-work of doubtful parentage, which had names all of their own. The pride of my undergraduate life, and later too, was a sort of deep-faced mashie known as the 'Benny', invented by and named after Ben Sayers, of North Berwick.

My father's dubious sixteen handicap was based largely on a sort of scuffling club known as the 'Chiper', which, rightly or wrongly, he pronounced to rhyme with 'viper'. Presumably if they had meant it as a club for chipping with they would have called it a 'Chipper', but he made it sound much more crafty as a 'Chiper'. My father also used another most descriptive expression that seems to have gone out of the game. Half-way through the downward swing, sensing that no good was going to come of it, he would exclaim, 'Ach! Smudged him!' It strikes me that, whatever they may now call themselves, a great many Smudgers are with us still. Roses by any other name . . .

The survey, as I mentioned, showed that 43 per cent of players (all of them subscribers to the magazine) had had their clubs for only two years or less. A previous survey conducted by Golf Monthly among readers in general showed no fewer than 59 per cent, to whose number I hope shortly to be added, since I have acquired a set of clubs which, as a reluctant concession to advancing years, are lighter and have a little 'give' in the shaft.

I suspect, as a matter of fact, that nearly all of us could do with lighter clubs. I picked up Christie O'Connor's brassie the other day and found it surprisingly light. Peter Thomson won the Open at Lytham driving throughout with a similar club, and I remember that muscular Frenchman J. Ado winning a long-driving competition at Frankfurt by about forty yards—the spectators having all had to be moved back before he was permitted to fire off. It transpired that he had mislaid his own driver and had borrowed one from a lady standing by.

British club design was, of course, much influenced by American just after the war, when new clubs over here were non-existent. My present irons were acquired in America at that time—since which the manufacturers have put out heaven knows how many new models of revolutionary and unparalleled superiority. When the managing director and the champion whose name my irons bear were here a year or two ago, I mentioned these clubs. Glancing cautiously around, they admitted, 'Yes. As a matter of fact we have never made anything to touch them since.'

Of one thing I am reasonably sure. Whereas American wooden clubs were designed to strike the larger ball, sitting up on strong, thick-bladed grass, our problem here is to get at a smaller ball crouching defiantly in thinner grass or on the clipped fairways of seaside links. The problems are not the same, and I still declare that the man who designs some really shallow-faced wooden clubs (such as I had for twenty years, designed by J. O. Lovelock at Mildenhall) could not only make a killing but would also benefit mankind.

The shallow face was, of course, the secret of that other maid-of-all-work, probably the easiest club to play with in the whole history of golf, the Jigger—something between a 4- and 5-iron in modern terms and virtually foolproof as a runner-up from doubtful distances. Some years ago my racing colleague, Roger Mortimer, kindly unearthed one for me but it got altered, or the head got exchanged, while being fitted with a new shaft. Can any veteran reader lay hands on one and pass it on to a guaranteed good home?*

* More than fifty correspondents offered jiggers and seven actually sent them. They confirmed what I said about its having been the easiest club in the bag.

ONCE YOU'VE HAD 'EM, YOU'VE GOT 'EM

The news from America that the great Sam Snead has won the Teacher Senior tournament using a croquet-mallet putter will bring to those of us who rely on the same kind of instrument, and for the same reason, a mixture of sympathy and apprehension. There can be little doubt that both in theory and in practice it is easier to line up a putter with two eyes facing squarely towards the hole than by peering at it sideways with one.

Mr R. D. Smyth, a member of the Berkhamsted club, who has christened his particular version of the croquet-putter the 'Binocular' (though this is not of course the only one—I have a fine brass specimen bearing the name of W. J. Cox), has lent strength to his theories not only by holing three ten-yarders running, on purpose, for the benefit of television but also by proving that a person of average eyesight, looking squarely at it, in other words 'binocularly', can detect a picture on the wall to be out of line by a quarter of one degree.

Almost every professional, and indeed almost every top-class amateur, who has tried croquet-putting, i.e. between the legs instead of the orthodox sideways manner, has marvelled at the ease with which putt after putt can be holed, or at any rate made to lodge so close as eventually to put the opponent off by casting doubt on his own method. Only one thing has kept them from adopting it— namely the fear of ridicule and, what is even worse, of being classed with such characters as former captains of the Royal and Ancient and chairmen of the Championship and Rules of Golf Committees, to say nothing of myself, of all of whom it is known that they putt with a croquet mallet not because they want to but solely on account of L.M.F.

For the benefit of younger readers, these singular letters were applied to wartime participants who, after a surfeit of dismantling land-mines of hitherto unknown design or flying out-of-date bombers a hundred times running over Germany, eventually went round the bend and were dismissed on the ground of 'Lack of Moral Fibre'. Their peacetime equivalents are those of us who, for a stake of half a crown or less, become twitching, blithering idiots when faced with moving a small piece of ironmongery to and fro in order to shift a small stationary ball into a comparatively large hole some two and a half feet away.

Snead, one of the most beautiful swingers of all times, so 'natural' that in his native Hill-Billy country of Virginia he once cut a wooden club out of the forest and with this and a putter went round in 76, got what they call in America the 'yips' some years ago. He appeared to get over them—or so the world thought—but the victim knew in his heart, as we all do, that 'once you've had 'em, you've got 'em'.

It is gratifying to some of us to know that this dread and ridiculous disease is not necessarily traceable to a dissolute way of life. Trying desperately for his fifth Open Championship about ten years ago, the Iron Man of golf himself, Ben Hogan, missed from three feet on the 71st green and lost by a stroke. In effect, this closed his competitive career—not because he missed the putt, which anyone could do, but because, for the first time in his life, he had 'yipped' it.

I hope soon to be watching him again in the Masters tournament at Augusta. Every green will be surrounded by spectators, some of them camping out there all day, and, as the familiar white-capped figure steps through the ropes, all will spontaneously rise and give him a standing ovation. A minute or two later he will be stuck motionless over the ball as though hypnotized, unable to move the ironmongery to and fro. Eventually, with a stiff, jerky movement reminiscent of those little men in the slot-machines on the pier, he will do so, and thousands who have been suffering silently in sympathy will wipe their brows with relief.

The 'twitch', as we tend to call it in this country, comes stealthily in the night and strikes down the best of men when, so to speak, they are not looking. Bill Cox tells—and such tales have an awful fascination for those of us who are afflicted—of how he was playing in a tournament before the war at Hesketh, Southport, partnered by that great player, Charles Whitcombe, a member of many a Ryder Cup team and captain of one.

At the last hole, into a tremendous wind, Whitcombe took a driver for his second and fired a low, boring shot which Cox remembers to this day. It nearly hit the stick and finished ten feet past. Whitcombe's first putt shot past the hole, almost as far again, and with his next one his putter stabbed into the ground. When at last he had holed out, he turned quietly and palely to Cox and said, 'I shall never in my life play in a tournament again'. And he never did.

My esteemed colleague, Leonard Crawley, whose exploit in so far misjudging his second shot at the last hole at Brookline, Mass., as actually to hit the Walker Cup on the lid, like a coconut, is not so widely known as it should be, will forgive my including him in our collection of ex-twitchers. I am not being beastly when I say that he may perhaps have looked down a little on our pathetic company, until out of a blue Italian sky at Monza ten years ago the bolt fell and added him to our number.

Having informed the authorities that he would not in any case be playing on the final day, he set out completely free of tension and

I

delighted to be drawn with Flory van Donck, then in his European prime. He hit his second shot to the first hole within nine feet and we may imagine the diffident clearing of the throat, the straightening of the tie, and the thought that all was well in the best of all worlds.

'It was not until I began to go through the normal motions to strike my first putt that I realized I had "got 'em" at last . . . I felt completely paralysed and in the course of the most appalling round of 85 shots I took 46 putts.' He put it down to a bilious attack, but in the second round it was worse. Then, on the first green at Rye in the President's Putter, he took four putts and 'decided to give up golf and let it become just a pleasant memory of the past'.

However, a chance meeting with one of our most senior members, a lifelong 'case' so severe as to merit anonymity, saved his reason and his golf and he is now virtually the unofficial president of the Croquet Club.

We welcome Snead to our number. He will bring unprecedented distinction to our ragged ranks, but in his presence I foresee danger. He has not joined us before, he says, because, 'Ah thought ah'd git laughed right off the course.' Now that he has proved it to be no laughing matter, someone else may get in on the act and may go and win the Open—and then where shall we be? I see the Rules of Golf Committee, meeting solemnly to decide whether our miserable mallet 'conforms to the traditional form and shape of golf clubs', and, before we know where we are, we shall find ourselves banned and back in the loony bin of golf. The only thing will be, I suppose, just as in some parts of India you have to register as an alcoholic to get a bottle of whisky, to claim exemption with the Royal and Ancient as 'registered twitchers'.

BEAUTY TREATMENT FOR GOLF

A letter of mine drawing attention to the fact that we in Sussex are to be treated to unlimited night flights from Gatwick on the ground that the airport is 'under-utilized', has brought me into touch with a correspondent whose nocturnal hours may also be rendered hideous by the incessant passage of package tours over his chimney-pots. Another who feels that, even if we cannot win, we may at least fire a few despairing shots at the Vulgarians before we give in, is Dr P. C. Harthoorn, of Cooden, whose son, he tells me, is the world's expert on putting down elephants with poisoned darts.*

Some while ago the good doctor (of Economics) was much incensed to find a man armed with a more normal weapon trying to shoot rather smaller fry, in the shape of the only pair of mallard living on the Cooden Beach golf course. As a result he now comes up with an idea which I hope may stimulate the imagination of golfing readers in the same way as it has been stimulating mine. What a wonderful thing, he suggests, if we all proclaimed our golf courses as Nature Reserves.

Years ago, when rural England was safe and beautiful and one could wake each morning secure in the knowledge that one's village home had not been surreptitiously designated by some anonymous planner as the centre of a new city for a quarter of a million people, such a suggestion would have been superfluous. Now, as the country-side vanishes and the beaches become caravan camps, it is nice to feel that golfers might do something to redress the balance—and the more ugly the surroundings in which they find themselves having to play, the greater can be their contribution.

Bird life is, of course, largely a matter to be detected and appreciated by experts, though every club lucky enough to possess a pond or lake should surely bring it to life with a few ornamental water fowl. I have a film of the swans waddling about on the edge of the 16th green at Pine Valley and it delights me every time I see it. So do the deer wandering on the fairways at Cypress Point and the sea-lions bobbing and barking on the rocks—so long as the wind is not blowing in from their direction—but we should not perhaps set our sights as high as deer and sea-lions to begin with.

What we want is colour. This is not an original thought on my part: it was Castlerosse's ambition, well before the war, to create the course at Killarney in full colour. Here, of course, man was much helped by Nature and by the proximity of the Gulf Stream, but, if

* But see 'Bleeding Pieces of Earth', p. 124.

you strike a sunny day in May or early June, when everything seems to be in flower at once, Killarney is indeed a sight to be seen.

Some clubs in England, too, have it laid on for them by nature. At Saunton, for instance, John Goodban, who played three times for Cambridge in the late thirties and is now secretary there, reckons that they have on the links nearly seventy-five per cent of the flowers illustrated in the Rev. Keble Martin's remarkable *Concise British Flora*. When the ladies held their county finals there in July, he had no difficulty in finding forty different specimens which he laid out on a dish for their edification. He also reckons that the area of divots hacked out each year works out at between a quarter and a third of an acre at each hole—but that is another story.

It is the more pedestrian sort of courses that really need the treatment and here we must look mainly to trees and shrubs—though bluebells, primroses and even violets, which grow wild in the few remaining bunkers at Huntercombe, are not to be despised. It so happens that my mind is full of all this and at any moment I am liable to toss in a whole stream of Latin names, memorized, if my friends but knew, only yesterday from the catalogue of Mr Geoffrey Goatcher, whose nurseries near my home are much admired.

The two acres which I have the honour to occupy are, together with the Pyecombe golf course, the only visible part of what used to be the South Downs not yet ploughed up, turned into prairie and wired off by farmers. The 'cramming' I have been doing on the subject of flowering shrubs, however, convinces me how much can be done in my little oasis—and the thought that it ought to have been done long ago makes me all the more eager to square my conscience by passing on the message.

I was encouraged, on going over to pick Mr Goatcher's brain, to find that there can be no golf course in the entire country that cannot be beautified by trees and shrubs which will 'do' in any form of soil, many of them with flowers in spring and berries in autumn. He quoted the viburnum family, cotoneaster, crabapples, mountain ash, berberis, dogwoods (I have a wonderful red one which glows in the winter sun but I gather that the yellow is outstanding too), forsythias, willows, and poplars. All these, it seemed, were only a beginning.

Even a single fir tree somehow lifts a course out of the 'meadow' class. Those lucky enough to have sandy soil can go in for the gold, yellow and green 'ornamental' conifers; mallow, which grows six feet in six months and flowers all summer; gorse, broom and amelanchier, or snowy mespilus; Japanese maple and the spectacular—wait for it—*acer plantanoides*. All right then, Norway Maple. He also mentioned lupins, and this at once set me in mind of Para-

paraumu in New Zealand which was ablaze with lupins when I was there.

Theirs 'go back' to yellow, ours to mauve, but what matter? Either would be a lovely sight growing wild on a golf course, though no good to me and my chalk. For myself, I am doing my best with broom, having purloined a whole pocketful of seed from Gleneagles during their October tournament. Like its new owner, however, it seems somewhat slow in germinating.

Another of my experiments has been an effort to create a butterfly sanctuary—all forms of such useless life having long ago been sprayed into extinction on the Downs. It has not been wholly unsuccessful, though I fear that a gale blew my puss moth and poplar hawk caterpillars off the Balsam Poplar I had planted specially for them, but it does remind me that every golf course could so easily be enlivened by the many varieties of buddleia and their attendant swarms of butterflies.

I had imagined that nothing much could be done on windy seaside links. Not at all. Escallonias, tamarisks, 'anything with grey foliage' will do well, said Mr G. 'Right in the spray,' he added.

It is not for me to preach, but it does seem that in all this there may be a thought for the captain of any club whose course is not particularly well endowed by nature, and for individual members, for whom the giving of a tree would be so pleasant a way of having their memory kept alive.

To many clubs it will not, of course, be new. It is many years, for instance, since at my home club at Bedford a planting programme was approved and there appeared overnight a modest plantation in the rough at the second. Next morning two retired Indian Army colonels, after fuming for some time on the tee, were observed to be brandishing their drivers and shouting, 'Fore.' They thought it was a four-ball looking for a ball.*

* Since that time the results have been fantastic. Anyone interested in seeing what can be done with a once bare 100-acre meadow should pay a visit to the Bedfordshire Golf Club.

BLEEDING PIECES OF EARTH

Writing of the train of thought set in mind by Dr P. C. Harthoorn, of Cooden, namely, to turn our golf courses into oases of natural beauty in an increasingly barren land, I added lightly that his son was the 'world's expert on putting down elephants with poisoned darts'. This, according to a correspondent who knows him well, does less than justice to what is clearly a remarkable man. 'What he has done', his friend writes, 'is to perfect the technique of immobilizing and tranquillizing large wild animals with the aid of the so-called "anaesthetic" dart. This new technique saves many animal lives and Tony Harthoorn has been called the Dr Schweitzer of the animal world. The present BBC television series *Daktari* is based on his work and he is the original "Daktari".' I make this correction with both interest and pleasure.

The theme of conserving the flora and fauna of our golf courses seems to have a wide, if not unanimous, approval. A lady whose garden abuts the 15th at Royal Wimbledon, for instance, says it is all very well but what about the foxes which not only do their courting in the bunkers, leaving some shocking lies in the morning, but have eaten her hens. They have also, it appears, eaten the last remaining pheasants, of which the members were rather proud.

Another correspondent says I need not go as far as New Zealand to find yellow lupins on a golf course. I have only to look from the second or third holes at St Andrews, across the New Course to the far side of the Jubilee, to see them in profusion, 'thrown out, no doubt, by local golfers'—though why good Scotsmen should go all that way to throw away free lupins is not stated.

My erstwhile foursomes partner in the University match at Royal St George's, Sandwich, H. Martin Row, informs me that he was playing there one day when they were accompanied for the first few holes—I will not give away how many—by a lady with a shopping-bag. Polite inquiry revealed that she was in search of asparagus and would get 'easily enough for four'. It was very good, apparently, and 'needed no salt in cooking'—though why that should be a virtue I cannot say.

As to the idea of members presenting trees to beautify their course and perpetuate their own memory, I seemed to remember once receiving a letter from Mr Gabs Kfouri, whom I had first met on the completely grassless course at Khartoum many years ago, when he was the founder of the milk supply of that infragrant city. It was about a scheme by which members were to present trees at the Brokenhurst Manor Club in the New Forest, on whose committee he was serving in his retirement. Following this up, I have to report in it a trap for the unwary.

About fifty trees were planted, the secretary tells me, but a certain lack of planning prevailed. Members chose their own trees. Some of these did not match in with the forest; others, indeed most, did not like the soil and lay down and died. Still, the idea is none the worse for that and it only remains to be guided by the local expert. And don't, says Mr C. K. Cotton, the golf architect, let him plant chestnuts or lime since you can't find your ball under the leaves in autumn. Advice from the Forestry Commission, he adds, has the merit of being 'unbiased, expert and free'.

A lively interest seems also to have been aroused by the *cri de coeur* from John Goodban, the secretary at Saunton, to the effect that members and visitors between them play about 60,000 rounds a year and in the course of it hack away between a quarter and a third of an acre at every hole. At short holes, he reckons, they destroy the equivalent of a whole tee forty by forty yards. The greenkeepers do their best to catch up, but most of the damage is done in the three or four months of summer.

Godban's calculations are based on a divot nine inches by three. When I suggested this to be a little on the large size, the reply was, 'Yes, but some of 'em take two!' Furthermore, a big proportion are liable to be carved out of the same small area where the drives finish. This is particularly true of the Old Course at St Andrews, where at several holes—the 7th is a good example—the undulations tend to 'gather' shots into the same small hollow, which often seems to consist more of divot marks than of grass.

Is Goodban right in suggesting that golfers no longer obey as they used to do those cardinal rules of etiquette: to replace divots and to smooth out their footmarks in bunkers? On the whole I suspect that he is—possibly because of so many newcomers to the game who have not been brought up, as I was as a boy, with the fear that, if you were seen not replacing a divot, you might get a frightful wigging from some elderly member or even be suspended from the club.

The tale is told at Saunton, incidentally, of the fiery member who stalked in with an enormous divot and, laying it on the bar in front of some luckless individual, said, 'Yours, sir, I believe.'

I also suspect that the taking of great divots was never part of the expert golfer's technique in earlier times. I cannot believe, for instance, that the great master, Harry Vardon—so accurate, it was said, that if he took a divot in the morning he was liable to land on it again in the afternoon—ever ploughed up the course as people do today, or that Taylor, the acknowledged master of the mashie, did the same damage with it as do players with its modern equivalent, the 6-iron.

On the other hand it seems certain that, despite (or even because of) chemicals and fertilizers and the increasing knowledge of the 'agronomists', courses are more lush than they used to be, especially at the seaside. The whole point of the celebrated 17th, or Road Hole, at St Andrews was that you had to play out to the right so as to leave a run-up over firm, dry ground to a fast green—a little too bold and you were over and down into the road, possibly for a long, long time: a little too timid and the ball would catch the slope and roll ignominiously down into the bunker.

Nowadays this approach is more like a meadow and, if you attempt a run-up, your ball is quite likely to get caught up in thick grass at the bottom of the bank. This sort of thing seems common to nearly all the great seaside courses. At Saunton, for instance, there appeared so many daisies that they were faced with the agonizing decision to use a spray, which was certain to destroy the wild thyme as well.

All this lends itself to the 'brute-force-and-ignorance' type of shot which hacks enormous pieces from the bleeding earth, and the time has perhaps come to try the remedy suggested at Saunton—namely, to pin up the biggest specimens on a board with the perpetrators' names attached, rather as a gamekeeper exhibits the remains of other destructive miscreants. Or, better still, to pick out of divot marks without penalty, quoting Rule 32 relating to 'cast or runway made by a burrowing animal'.

H.S.——E.O.B.——S.B.——F.T.——D.B.A.B.F.!

Comparing the heroes of yesterday with those of today is a tempting, if fruitless, pastime. When Ben Hogan won the British Open in 1953, it so happened that on his return Bobby Jones was in New York and they sat together at a celebratory luncheon. Jones said he was embarrassed at stories comparing the merits of the two of them, to which Hogan replied, 'You may be sure I understand. I have always felt and said that a man who could be a champion in one era could be a champion in any other, because he has what it takes to get to the top.'

Jones himself has written what has often seemed to me the final word on this everlasting, though still intriguing, topic of 'Was Young Tom Morris as good as John Ball, as good as Vardon, as good as Jones, as good as Hogan, as good as Palmer?' He said simply, 'All that a man can do is to beat the people who are around at the same time that he is. He cannot win from those who came before, any more than he can from those who come afterward.'

Nevertheless, the seeds of doubt flourish in my own mind and *Golf in Six Lessons*, a little book kindly sent to me by a reader, recalls a long-standing belief that you can judge the comparative capabilities of generations of golfers very well by what they teach and what they themselves think they do. I know that courses and clothes and balls and clubs, particularly the shafts, were different, and I know that high-speed photography has now shown golfers often to be doing something different from what they thought they were doing—though I am not sure that in the end I would not rather know what they felt they were doing than what they were, if you see what I mean.

Golf in Six Lessons, undated, was one of a series on sports and pastimes and, judging by the demonstrator's boots, cap, and plus-fours and by the phrase, 'We may take it that the famous player, Havers, is consistently the longest driver we have' (Havers won the Open in 1923), I should put it at just after the First World War. With the Great Triumvirate of Vardon, Braid and Taylor no longer in the hunt and with Hagen and Jones already on the scene, we can think of that era in terms of 'modern' golf.

The instruction in these pages, however, compared with what is known today, is manifestly grotesque. In 'addressing the ball', for instance, you cock the club up with the wrists, forward and past the ball till it is pointing directly upwards in front of you, and in the second movement you cock it up vertically behind you, in a position identical with 'backswing for the Half Iron'. In both cases the fingers of the left hand have completely let go—the piccolo grip in its most malignant form.

The art of putting, one might think, would remain common ground, since the basic problem has hardly changed. Here again the author tells us how—and I invite anyone subject to the 'yips' not to risk his sanity by reading any further. 'Take the putter back slowly for about a yard and, as it comes forward, sway the body towards the hole as you strike the ball. This enables you to judge at the very last moment what power you must put into the stroke.' From the very act of writing it down I doubt whether I shall sleep tonight!

It being perhaps unfair to judge by so humble a publication, I have been turning to the former masters, in particular J. H. Taylor, who became resident instructor, so to speak, to the opening numbers of C. B. Fry's magazine in 1904. Having already won the Open three times, he may be taken as gospel. Yet the very kindest thing one could call his outlines of the golf swing, as illustrated, would be 'workmanlike'.

'J. H.' was a great advocate of the open stance, in some cases with the left toe at least a foot behind the right and pointing almost at the hole. One picture shows footprints in the snow, for mashie shots of ninety, seventy and fifty yards—six prints in all, addressing the same ball. The three stances are equally 'open', but his left foot is farthest in front of the ball for the longest of the three and almost level with it for the shortest. See any book by any present-day instructor for precisely the opposite.

Taylor said that, if he stood square to the ball—see Peter Thomson, Joyce Wethered, John Jacobs et al—his right elbow went up and away from the body in the backswing and that this was wrong. The fact that many experts were illustrated with the right elbows 'up' was held in those days to be due to a natural tendency while holding so awkward a pose.

In the case of the young lady on the mantelpiece of the Dormy House at Rye this is understandable, since it must have taken many a long sitting—or standing. She will have been fortified, I am sure, by the thought that she was, and probably for ever would be, the only member of her sex to be rendered in bronze at the top of the backswing stark naked—and for the pleasure she has given generations of undergraduates, to say nothing of their elders, the more power to her elbow wherever it points.

Nearly all the experts of these early days show themselves—and it cannot always be due to fatigue in posing for the camera—with the club almost dropping on to their shoulders at the top of the swing. This includes Mr Stuart Morrison, founder and Manager of the Golf School at the Royal Botanic Gardens, Regent's Park, who has by this time given between 25,000 and 30,000 lessons (*Strand Magazine*,

1912, concurrent with instalment four of Conan Doyle's *The Lost World*).

Film strips of today's champions show them to be able to hit their longest shots without moving their heads in the process—unless it be slightly backwards. Taylor, shown against a trellis-like background of twelve-inch squares, bobs his head down at least six inches. Horace Hutchinson reaches almost a kneeling position at the top of the swing. Harold Hilton, twice Open Champion, finishes a drive leaning forward with his head so far beyond his left foot that another few inches must topple him over.

Here at least the author of the *Six Lessons* seems in advance of his time, and convinces me that we must at once go back to wooden shafts. It is essential, he says, for the head to remain still and 'to keep this constantly before you, it is a good plan for the beginner to put the letters H.S., for Head Still, on every shaft just below the grip'. I cannot wait for my new driver with the shaft carved like a totem pole: H.S.——E.O.B.——S.B.——F.T.——D.B.A.B.F., and numerous others, scarcely repeatable in these respectable columns.

SAFER TO SIT IN THE CLUBHOUSE

Years ago in the eighties, in a little book on his golfing life at St Andrews, W. T. Linskill, generally remembered, though possibly inaccurately, as the 'founder of Cambridge Golf', ridiculed the current public supposition that golf was a dangerous game—adding almost casually that he himself had 'certainly not been struck more than three times this season'. The Old Course was then, I fancy, only forty or fifty yards wide at some points and they used the same narrow track outwards and inwards, with only one hole on each green, constantly playing at, through, and into each other.

Researches following a recent law case show in fact that golf is, or has become, one of the most dangerous games in the world, the hazards to life and limb far exceeding those of such sports as prize-fighting and Rugby football. The case itself has shown, further, that each one of us had better get out a magnifying-glass with which to scrutinize his golfer's insurance.

I had thought, as so many innocent citizens do in so many walks of life, including those who carry passengers in motor cars, that as a golfer I was insured for 'everything'. The case in question proves very much to the contrary. It arose from the present captain of the Shirley Park Golf Club, Mr Raymond Delo, having delivered a stroke so wayward as he had deemed impossible and his ball having struck the then captain, Mr Sidney Brewer, with most unhappy consequences, in the eye. Both were insured.

It now transpires that the injured party cannot obtain compensation unless, by litigation, he can prove negligence on the part of the other. The case was to decide whether Mr Delo was 'negligent', and Mr Justice Hinchcliffe (handicap twenty) decided that he was not. Mr Brewer was therefore left with a badly injured eye, no compensation, and 'damages' of £1,000, i.e. £500 in income-tax to the Government for earning the £1,000 and the other £500 to the lawyers by whose leisurely processes the case had taken two and a half years to reach the court.

'To no one will we sell, deny or delay justice.' (Magna Carta, 1215.)

'Even if the damage was foreseeable,' said the judge, in words which I can see being taken down and used in evidence for many a long day, 'the possibility of injury occurring involves a risk so small that a reasonable man would feel justified in disregarding it.'

How small does the possibility have to be? In some tournaments I have watched it seems not so much a possibility as a certainty. Balls pitch continually into masses of spectators, occasionally knocking one down like a ninepin, often miraculously not. Sometimes they are

standing so close to the target that it must surely be at their own risk.
At others they are where the stewards have told them, and it must
surely in this case be the player who is negligent if he bombards them—
their proximity involving 'a risk so great that no reasonable man would
feel justified in disregarding it'.

Yet I doubt whether they would get any compensation. In any case,
all that most of them do on regaining consciousness is to apologize for
getting in the way! The principle seems to be *Caveat Spectator*.

Nevertheless, it makes you think. When I drive off the 1st tee at
St Andrews, I know perfectly well that I am liable to slice on to the
public putting-green, or off the 18th into the crowded road or even
into somebody's window—in fact one such stroke, mercifully not of
mine, did cause the death of a seventy-year-old lady in 1940.

At Rye I suppose there is not a single member who has not at some
time pitched on the Camber road (600 cars an hour in summer) from
the tenth. Over the whole country such instances of potentially
dangerous driving must run into thousands. Perhaps the answer is that
we knew so damned well that we should probably do it that there
would be no doubt in the injured party proving our 'negligence' and
therefore being able to claim from our insurance.

Mr Brewer, the injured party at Shirley Park, of whom happily it is
reported that an operation may restore the sight of his eye, may take
sombre consolation from the thought that it might have been worse.
Mr Jimmy de Rothschild, the former Liberal MP, racehorse-owner
and multimillionaire, who died ten years ago at the age of seventy-
eight, was playing at Deauville just after the First World War when a
ball struck his monocle and cost him his eye.

A golfer on a Welsh course, having played from a bunker, jumped
up to see the result and by a fantastic coincidence was at that moment
hit on the back of the head by a ball from behind. Within a week he
was totally blind.

A Scottish golfer, on finding an old ball—it must have been a very
old ball—decided to drive it away off the course. It hit a wall, re-
bounded and knocked out one eye of his opponent. Indeed, there
seems no limit to the misfortunes that can befall people on golf courses.
Perhaps the earliest on record is that of the local schoolmaster in East
Wemyss, Fife, who in 1748 was hit on the leg by one of the old
'feathery' balls—and had to have it amputated. In later times a man was
struck on the leg and died from the blood clot that formed as a result.

The number of causes from which people have died on the links—
resulting from a risk 'so small that no reasonable man ...' etcetera—is
to me astonishing. Many have been boys—including one who was
merely pottering round on a municipal putting-course—though in

one case it was the father. He had been giving his son some instruction but the boy missed the ball and caught the father on the temple. Innumerable golfers have swung the club back in disgust after a bad shot and severely injured, and in at least one case killed, their partner. It has even happened in the Amateur Championship.

Death strikes in a multitude of ways, including of course by lightning and falling trees. Golfers have been killed through accident with golf carts; through walking across the railway line without looking—this must be negligence, one would have thought—and on two occasions through broken shafts piercing the body. Perhaps unluckiest of all were the two lady golfers in Florida who were walking innocently down the fairway when a navy fighter plane, coming silently in against the wind, out of control and with a dead engine, cut them to pieces with its propeller.

What with the early spring and the primroses coming out and my new clubs, I had intended to play this morning. On second thoughts it seems safer to sit in the clubhouse.

IF AT FIRST YOU DON'T SUCCEED

This is the time of year, 'now that April's here', when golfers, lured prematurely out of hibernation, like the tortoiseshell butterflies in the attic, by a single fine day, find themselves playing in the Easter club competitions and discover that, while they suspected they were bad, they never knew they could be quite as bad as that. Some hundreds of thousands will play this weekend in the form of club competition devised by and named after the immortal Dr Stableford, of Wallasey, who, if there had been knighthoods for golf, should assuredly have had one—not so much for the pleasure he has given as for the humiliations he has saved.

His form of competition gives two points for a bogey at each hole, one point for one over, three points for one under. The golfer is, therefore, spared the ignominy of admitting on return to the clubhouse from an ordinary stroke competition that his score was 102—10=92. He merely says he 'did not do very well; only got 16 points', which, seeing that he ought in theory to get 36, is much the same thing.

Bookmakers are not only, many of them, enthusiastic golfers, but are showing a tendency to wager on the game as well. Would any of my friends in the fraternity, I wonder, care to take me up on the results of club competitions over Easter? 'For every score better than 36, I give you £10. For every 36, I give you £5. For every card lower than 36, you give me 5s.' I reckon that any of them who took this on would be back to the grindstone, while I, tossing a few consolatory thousands to the tax-collector, could retire to the sun.

So much for our handicaps. Why are so many of us so bad at this time of year? Is it only the stiffened muscles of winter? I have been making certain investigations and, though I cannot come up with anything startlingly new, I may have something to offer. Those who can play to their handicaps need read no farther.

Some time ago Henry Cotton, casting an eye over my twenty-year-old iron clubs, made approving comments, to which I replied modestly that the manufacturers had in fact admitted them to be the best they had ever designed. 'But of course,' he added, 'it's no use trying to play with them like that.' The 'like that' referred to the grips which, despite occasional doses of castor oil and raspings with a file, were hard, cold and shiny and caused most of my shots, when I managed to keep hold of the club, to sting abominably.

I took them to the young professional at a near-by club and ordered nine new grips. As a matter of interest, I asked, how much would it be? 'Eighteen shillings,' he said. 'Now, look,' I replied in my best avuncular way. 'You'll never get rich like that. We expect to pay you the proper rate for the job.' He looked at me a little blankly; then the penny dropped. He meant eighteen shillings each. Last time I had a grip put on, it was half a crown. Nowadays, I believe, you can revive them with a kind of spray.

What 'goes' first in the professional golfer, according to Cotton, is the legs. In us part-timers I cannot help thinking it is the hands. Anyone who finds it not quite so easy as it used to be to unscrew the tops of bottles, jam-jars or his good lady's nail-varnish-remover will, I am sure, agree. If the hands are not strong enough to take charge of the swing, the body will. See any 1st tee any Sunday morning.

Next to go, and therefore to be somehow restored, is one's concentration, and particularly concentration in the right place. I have often thought of producing a sort of 'graph of intensity', an outline of the golf swing with the thickness of the line varying with the degree of concentration. The professional, I suspect, would show a very thick line at the start, thinning out over the first two feet, vanishing altogether after three, then reappearing about where it vanished, thickening strongly before impact and for three feet after the ball, and then disappearing.

For the average club golfer you would also have to show the waggles as he addressed the ball, since these would produce the thickest lines of all. Here he is thinking hardest, where the professional is hardly thinking at all. On the backswing his line continues thick, if anything getting thicker, until very nearly the top, where suddenly, inexplicably, it vanishes altogether, never to re-appear. At this moment the ball disappears from his eye and he remembers nothing more. The slower the backswing, the 'thicker' very often the concentration— and the more instantly it vanishes as the downward snake-killing slash begins. I have often suspected this ancient golfing adage of 'slow back' to be an illusion. Watching, for instance, Harry Weetman clouting the ball one feels it would be just as painful to be struck on the backswing as on the forward. Now, however, by a curious chance I know for a certainty the answer.

It may be remembered that the BBC filmed a number of golf matches, each of which took anything up to ten hours on the course, every shot being filmed by quite a number of cameras. The process of editing this mass of material down to fifty minutes per film draws now, I am happy to say, towards its painstaking end. I have been called upon from time to time to attend and, since we so often have had to retrace our steps in the film, have now seen the great men of golf play at least a hundred tee-shots in reverse.

First impressions astonish me. Starting from a point, say, half-way through the follow-through and going backwards (the ball suddenly appearing on the way), they flash the club back with a loud *phwit* reminiscent of more painful moments at school; at the top of the swing they pause, and then slowly, very slowly, place the club down behind the ball—this being, of course, the original backswing. The visual impression is that at the moment of impact the club is travelling at least five times as fast, though an electronic eye might, for all I know, show it to be ten or twenty.

It took me some time before I discovered the secret. They flashed the club back at immense speed (still in reverse) from where the club was horizontal in front of the ball to the same position behind and you could not follow the clubhead. Then suddenly they slowed up before they got to the top—this, right way round, being the beginning of the downswing. So the answer, once and for all, is that they do go 'slow back' but they also go, and for quite a long way, 'slow down'.

I remember not only Peter Thomson but also John Jacobs, each making the best of a bad job, rubbing into me the fact that a club placed across one's chest, as one addressed the ball, should be pointing at the hole. I also remember the late Reg Whitcombe, his huge left hand grasping a niblick, practising one-handed swings in his shop. 'Your hand should always finish covering the flag,' he said, this presumably being the logical result of the club pointing at the hole.

I accordingly got myself correctly 'set up' on the Downs yesterday, facing the sea, with the club across my chest pointing squarely at the left-hand chimney of the Shoreham Power Station. A moment later I was posing on the follow-through to study the position of my hands, only to find them obscuring not the Shoreham Power Station but the grandstands of Brighton Racecourse on top of the hill five miles to the left. Never mind. If at first you don't succeed . . . by the end of the next practice session I hope at least to be covering the hideous new block of flats midway between the two.

K

YOU CAN'T LET THEM DO IT, BARBARA!*

My curious and occasionally envied way of life involves a considerable amount of travel, fortunately at his Lordship's expense, and this takes three forms. This week's, by air to Augusta for the Masters tournament via Washington, Atlanta and all points south, is the fastest but by far the most uncomfortable. It is now twenty-two years since the tailor at Olympia, thrusting a tape measure against my chest for my demob suit, turned to a colleague and announced in a loud voice, 'Forty-two, short, portly'. I fear that I have not decreased in the meantime, and to sit for seven hours crampled in a little seat, seeing nothing and in the end hearing practically nothing, is not my idea of heaven, even if I am being miraculously carried along at 500 m.p.h. in the process.

Aeroplanes at the moment go either too fast or not fast enough. Thus, on arrival at Augusta at what I am pleased to call 3.15 a.m. 'stomach-time' tomorrow, one sets the watch back six hours and calls it 9.15 p.m. today. This is not so bad, as one can soon retire to bed. On the way back, however, after a long day in America and most of the night in the aeroplane, one is brought down to earth at 3 a.m. 'stomach-time', only to be told that it is 9 a.m. and that a bright new day has just begun. Experience shows that one 'purple heart' will carry me over till lunchtime, after which the favourite drops in his tracks and is comparatively useless for two and a half days.

The second form of transport, though not across the Atlantic, is the motor car, of which I possess a notable specimen. It gives me conscious pleasure every time I get into it, but to sit in it for four days in order to get to Scotland and back, harried by maniacs and Minis, is, again, not my idea of heaven, though it might well lead to it. As a believer in the law of averages, I take the view that, if you expose yourself long enough, they're bound to get you in the end.

No, there is only one way to travel and that is by train. I have long known this and have more than once written of the good sober driver, the private butler and chef and, when necessary, the bedside attendant, with whom I like to be accompanied when I make my way about the country. The only trouble is that too many of the Philistines are beginning to cotton on to what was previously known only to connoisseurs. However, one may still remain 'one up' with a certain expertise.

They don't yet realize, fortunately, that you want to make a bee-line for a corner seat in a middle compartment (where you get waggled about less than in the end ones), back to the engine (so that the scenery flows away from you instead of at you) and, of course, non-smoking (in case someone lights up one of those ghastly little imitation cigars).

* Mrs Barbara Castle, the then Minister of Transport.

They don't even know to bring with them for the sleeper the pink pill and the cotton wool for the ears—which the airlines provide and the railway still don't—and to put the plug in the basin, up through which comes so much of the noise.

I am not the first of those who follow the golfing scene to write nostalgically of the sleeper to Scotland—the anticipatory dinner at the club; the bustling scene at Euston or King's Cross, with the sorters already at work in the great mail train and the nets now folded back on the sides, later to reach out in the night and grab new cargo as they pass; and, finally, the moment of waking in a new world of hillsides, burns, a dashing river and air like champagne.

Sometimes, as you look out over the last miles of uninhabited moorland before Gleneagles, you see skein after skein of geese in the sky. At Kilmarnock you may be forgiven the unworthy temptation, as the long row of sleepers trundles away, of thanking the Lord that you are not as other men are, since they are being taken on to Glasgow, while you are going to Ayr and thence over the coast road, past Culzean Castle and one of the noblest views in Britain, to Turnberry.

Supreme among journeys to Scotland, however, is that of the golfing pilgrim to Mecca, in other words St Andrews. I still cherish the bound volumes of *Railway Wonders of the World* collected as a boy, with the wonderful coloured picture of the express roaring over the Forth Bridge and, in order never to miss it, I have fallen into the way of catching the earlier train to Edinburgh and thence the breakfast train at 7.30 from platform 15, in which, almost as a ritual, I have finnan-haddock while crossing the bridge. There used also to be the Navy, with battleships looking like toys in the bath down below, but now there is the magnificent road bridge whose single span exceeds, unbelievably, the length of the two longest holes at St Andrews put together.

Soon we hear the familiar cry of, 'Leuchars. Change for St Andra's,' and we board the little two-carriage train waiting at the buffers between the two main lines. It used to be hauled by a veteran steam engine called the 'Kettledrummle', but now it is a diesel, which is better really because, by sitting up in front, you can see where you are going. For golfers from all the nations—and, I like to think, for many of the students in the ancient and ever-growing university—this is the most memorable train journey in the world.

Round the corner to Guard Bridge, past that fellow's immaculate vegetable garden and the paper mill, across the bridge over the Eden— the driver having already twice leaned out to exchange those big rings with leather pouches attached in order to secure his right of way— and alongside the estuary with, at low tide, its innumerable birds on

the mudflats. In the distance now the singular, unforgettable outline
of the 'Old Grey Town', with its spires and towers and the ruins of
the cathedral.

We pass on our left the far end of the Eden course and soon we are
hard beside the Old Course itself. The 16th tee is right against the
railway fence and so is the 17th, and on the farther side of the big
double greens the early starters are already on their way out. From
the train I once detected on the second a four-ball consisting of three
peers and a knight! Passing behind the black sheds over which you
drive at the Road Hole, we see the little Road bunker, in which every
great golfer has at some time stood, with the same thoughts running
through his head, and behind the green the dreaded road itself.

A quick glimpse of the Royal and Ancient clubhouse standing
foursquare behind the first tee and we are rounding the bend with a
cheerful toot to announce our arrival at the little station, where
dedicated hands have traced out on the bank in white stones the legend:
St Andrews. Home of Golf. The golfer is home indeed.

Soon more and more pilgrims will be coming to St Andrews,
for the railways are to replace the old black sheds and the coalyard,
into which we slice out of bounds at the 17th, with a magnificent half-
million-pound hotel.

In the meantime, quietly, almost furtively, and in very small print,
they propose—believe it or not, and you scarcely will—to abandon
the railway and close the station.

You can't let them do it, Barbara. You can't, really!

HORSES, POTWALLOPERS AND A MONKEY

A few days off in the West Country in pursuit of fish which, as usual, proved to be elsewhere, have seen me involved yet again in golf, firstly at Sidmouth, where I attended a public inquiry—most impressively conducted, I thought—into a controversy as to whether the council of that congenial little suntrap should build a golf course on the moor above the town to replace their present 5,000-odd-yard course, which is so hilly as to put middle-aged members in fear of heart attacks.

My allegedly expert evidence was to the effect that, if they decided to make a course on the moor, it must assuredly be a very good one and might prove superlative. I was surprised to find a spirited minority in opposition but, as it is no affair of mine, will leave it at that. The visit did, however, afford a pleasant diversion to call upon Sir John and Lady Heathcoat-Amory, who were runners-up in the 1948 Worplesdon Foursomes, she having already, as Joyce Wethered, won it eight times with seven different partners.

The greatest woman golfer of her time, perhaps of all time, now plays 'about a round and a half a year' and the skill she used to display on the golf course is devoted to the gardens of their lovely home near Tiverton. These are in full bloom just now and, being open to the public, should not be missed by anyone finding themselves within striking distance.

Less elevating to the spirit, indeed very much the opposite, was a visit to Westward Ho! Here is the oldest club in England still playing on its original links—it celebrated its centenary in 1964—and you never saw such a mess in all your life. The 1st, 2nd and 18th holes are a depressing shade of brown through the sea getting in twice in three weeks, but they will recover. The real trouble is animals.

The links of Westward Ho! lie—or is it 'lies'?—on a flat expanse of land known as the Burrows and protected from the sea by the great Pebble Ridge. This, though the point is quite irrelevant, was the schoolday background of Kipling's *Stalky and Co.* For a thousand years, or so it is claimed, the 'Potwallopers' of Northam—i.e. the locals; anyone who 'boils his pot' in the parish—have had the right to raise their animals on the Burrows and, though there is in fact plenty of room for the animals and the golfers to live apart, the grazing rights include the golf course. Naturally enough, these are jealously guarded. Nor are they disputed by the golfers.

Nowadays, however, comparatively few of the true potwallopers possess the animals which the rights originally assumed in the days of the peasants—the odd pig, cow and sheep etcetera—though a few do

keep a horse or perhaps a pony for the children. Instead commercial
operators in the shape of riding stables with horses for hire and full-
scale sheep-farmers have moved in upon the grazing. At the moment,
roaming over the historic links of Westward Ho! are no fewer than a
hundred horses and two thousand sheep.

Quite apart from the fact that the golfers have to contend with
sufficient horse manure to start the biggest mushroom farm in Britain,
the effect of the horses' hooves on the greens may well be imagined.
Sometimes a number of horses decide upon a jolly stampede right
across the course, the secretary wincing powerlessly as he watches from
the club veranda. Making good the damage done to the greens by
horses is the full-time labour of one man for the whole year. It has
now come to the stage, they said at the club, where it is 'either horses
or golf'. At the very best the golf, if combined with the horses, could
be only fourth-rate.

Greens can, of course, be repaired, but another aspect of the present
situation is rapidly becoming irreparable. One of the most celebrated
holes is the 4th, alongside the sand dunes, the hole where you have to
make the carry over what is almost certainly the biggest sleepered
bunker in England. Everyone who has played at Westward Ho! will
remember it. The part you have to carry, once crisp seaside turf, is
now deep in blown sand. As to the bunker, its outline has vanished
and sand is in places right up to the top of the sleepers. The fairway
area is now yellow, with occasional wisps of grass showing through,
and so is most of the neighbouring 15th. Golf is almost unplayable
now. Soon it will be completely unplayable. It breaks your heart to
look at it.

The secretary of the Burrows Committee, Mr Harold Ford, who
is a boat-builder in Northam and by definition, like many of the
golfers, a potwalloper, told me that the sudden appearance of the
sand might be due to the cars out at the Pebble Ridge, which at 2s. a
time bring £4,500 a year to the council, gradually encroaching and
loosening the sand, but, listening with what I hope to have been a
neutral ear and also inspecting the scene, I was more convinced by
the golfers' explanation that all was well for a hundred years until the
horses ate the marram grass which holds the sandhills together.

After all, it was the ubiquitous goat, nibbling away at the herbage,
which turned most of the once fertile Middle East into desert, and the
same thing has assuredly happened at Westward Ho! A short while
ago volunteers from the club, rather like their neighbours on the
oil-ridden beaches of Cornwall, solemnly swept the fourth fairway
with brooms and removed 150 cartloads of sand. They might as well
have swept the Sahara. Not to be beaten, however, they have now got

permission to fence off the 4th hole from the sandhills to keep the horses, though not the sheep, off them and today, this very morning, the members are due to march out and erect the fence for themselves rather than wait for someone else to do it.

On top of all this the club pays rates for the use of its part of the Burrows, while the sheep-farmers and the riding schools, one of which runs fifty horses over the links, pay nothing at all, relying on the ancient rights of the potwallopers. There are at least 200 acres, the golfers claim, in which the horses could be contained, and the local Chamber of Commerce would like to see a sort of Rotten Row on which young holidaymakers could be taught to ride.

I never thought to be writing in favour of a Ministry of Sport, but I am glad to say that Mr Denis Howell, the Minister, has directed the secretary of the S.W. Area Sports Council to go and meet the interested parties to try to sort the matter out. Mr Ford thought that some form of 'Commons Act' was due in five years' time and that this would take care of the problem. The only trouble is that in five years' time there will be no problem left to take care of.*

It is all rather tragic, but in order not to spoil your day I will end on a lighter note. Many will remember that distinguished-looking figure, H. R. Buckland, who sold and popularized a brand of whisky in almost every senior club in the country and with whom a friend told me last week he was once playing at Westward Ho! As they came up the 18th, Buckland felt his trolley to be pulling rather heavily and, on looking round, found a monkey sitting on his clubs.

One may imagine the swift glance back to the front, while he worked out whether he was seeing things, and the furtive backward glance again. It *was* a monkey, and it was still there. Its owner had brought it down to the beach in his car and it had escaped. When Buckland tried to dislodge it, it made hostile grimaces and bit him. Then it jumped to and fro over the brook in front of the last green and finished up on the club flagstaff, whence it was eventually lured down by the steward's son. True or false? They swear it is true, every word.

* Hope was restored some months later, by which time the 4th and 5th holes had been fenced off and the marram grass had begun to grow. A new dyke will take the sea water from the first two and last two holes, but the battle to save England's oldest course is not yet won.

MUCH GOLD—NO GOLDEN AGE

Golf today, particularly in America, is the biggest business in the history of games and pastimes, and those who reach the top become multi-millionaires, in such style as to turn green with envy those who played at least as well as they do, and in some cases better, but did it at the wrong time. The fortunate ones, however, are the merest tip of the iceberg. Behind them lies a truly colossal industry, selling, through their names, not only clubs, balls, clothing, and all the miscellaneous paraphernalia of golf, but insurance, laundries, par-3 courses, printing and even aeroplanes. Will this bubble ever burst? A recent visit to America convinced me that it certainly will not in the immediate future, but that people are beginning to suspect that every good thing has its limitations.

One detects these things only from casual conversational straws in the wind, so to speak, and in this way I gained an impression of resentment at the magnitude of the empire created by that most likeable of managers Mark McCormack, who started by handling one or two minor affairs for his schooldays companion Arnold Palmer, and, without suspecting it at the beginning, has ended in such a position that people are forecasting the time when you can't even run a championship without his permission. This, of course—no pun intended—is beyond the mark, but it is true that, if he did withhold his players, the result would be a championship only in name.

There is no doubt, too, that big business has eliminated the old cameraderie among the great players. You could hardly find a nicer fellow than Palmer, but he has no time, either physically or mentally—and little wonder. He was at one time president—or, as we should call it, chairman—of, I think, thirty-two companies, though he recently sold off some of these for a few millions to a television company, rather as Ian Fleming sold his copyrights to Booker Bros. Nevertheless, Palmer's life remains one of almost perpetual motion—golfing, hand-shaking, conferring, endorsing, being called to the telephone, acknowledging compliments, and, of course, since he owns an $800,000 jet aeroplane and is agent for the firm that makes it, finding time occasionally to go and fly the damned thing.

One of the old school, Gene Sarazen, was looking nostalgically back during the Masters Tournament to the Golden Age of golf in the late twenties and early thirties, of which he was so notable an ornament. This splendid, olive-skinned little man, always such a favourite in Britain—he was born Eugene Saraceni 'on the wrong side of the tracks', as they say in America—might be in his early fifties, but is in fact sixty-four. Holding the club two or three inches below the end of the grip, he still gives the ball the same simple, determined clout and, granted a clear course, will get round it in two and a quarter hours, by which time the modern experts will just be teeing off at the 9th. The day cannot be far distant when he goes round in his age—if indeed he has not already done so.

I mention this to show that Sarazen is by no means a retired yearner for the good old days. His heart, like Gary Player's, is in his farm— everyone calls him 'the Squire'—but he is active in golf and television and still makes a vast income from the game. One thing he does frankly regret, however, is that none of the champions of today has time to sit around and talk, and to meet the members of the clubs which play host to them, as he and his great hero and rival, Walter Hagen, made it their business and pleasure to do.

'Never worry,' Hagen used to say, 'never hurry. Always stop and smell the flowers.' It was this sort of thing, set off by the presence of that complete amateur, Bobby Jones, who generally beat them all, that made theirs the Golden Age. Nowadays there is fifty times as much gold, but it will never pass into history as a Golden Age.

Sarazen is by no means averse to change—indeed he is constantly getting his name in the papers as advocate of such heresies as the eight-inch golf hole, to neutralize the undue preponderance which putting plays in the game—but he will risk being called 'square' as well as Squire by standing up for the old against the new. I am happy to see that he has just been doing so in the American magazine *Golf*, on the subject of golf-course design. He thinks that much modern design is 'ridiculous'. So do I, but that does not matter.

Most new courses in America, or for American tourists overseas, form part of a real-estate deal, the idea being to sell plots of land around or near the perimeter, and nothing will do but a so-called 'championship' course. To us this means a course on which national championships are played. To them it means 7,000 yards.

'When someone tells me his course measures more than 7,000 yards, it is usually said with the pride of a new father, as if distance, or wasting a lot of land, is something to boast about. Water a course of that length from tee to green, brother, and you are playing a course equivalent to 8,000 or 9,000 yards when it is dry and when you aren't being robbed of your roll.' One of his principal 'beefs', he says, is the heavy watering which makes the fairways lush and the greens so sodden that no skill is needed to pitch on them and stop.

Another of his 'beefs' is the over-long short hole. 'Modern architects,' he declares, 'have forgotten the definition of a short hole. They boast of 225–50-yard backbreakers on which only the longest hitters can get home . . . anyone can lay out a 250-yard hole and call it a difficult

par-3.' It is not merely advancing years that makes me dislike these
very long 'everything to lose, nothing to gain' par-3 holes. I would
rather see a 'bad-length' par-4 of 270 or 280 yards with everything to
gain. The National Unions at home say that everything under 250
must be ruled a par-3—but how many people can hit a golf ball 250
yards? Five per cent? I doubt it.

We ourselves, I am happy to see, come in for praise. 'If you go to
Troon or Prestwick, or some of the other classic courses abroad, you
will see par-3s of from 140 to 150 yards, which will drive home the
idea, for they are designed for exquisite iron play and not a luck shot
with anything from a 4-wood to a driver.'

Of the 'postage stamp' hole at Troon, 120-odd yards to a tiny green
guarded by deep bunkers, Sarazen writes, 'I don't know what brand
of hair tonic you use but you'd better douse it on well, because this
hole will make your hair stand on end.'

Tomorrow I too hope to be in Scotland, playing, as it happens, on
the biggest greens in the entire world. Even so, you are bound to get
down to the four-footers in the end, and if the citizens of St Andrews
see a strange figure dousing on the hair tonic, they will know who it is,
and why.

CADDIE-MASTER EARNS LITERARY AWARD

Those familiar with the golfing scene around London, together with many a distinguished visitor from distant lands, will be aware that the caddie-master at Sunningdale is something of a 'character', and, even though, which is not impossible, they may have fallen out with him at first impact, a very considerable man in his own right. This is Sheridan, assuredly the only caddie-master to have had his portrait hung in the Academy, to have it now hanging on the clubhouse wall, and to have been elected an honorary member of the club. My favourite reading has always been other people's lives, and clearly there might be some interesting episodes in Sheridan's if someone could extract them from this forthright, monosyllabic Scot. Instead he has done it, I am assured, all for himself, and the result, *Sheridan of Sunningdale*, has given me hours of pleasure.

As with most autobiographies it is the early days which fascinate. Sheridan's father was evidently a genius with soil and livestock and was a farm manager in the East Lothians at eighteen. The son, however, did not take readily to life on the land. This was at the turn of the century, when a man with a guaranteed wage of one pound a week was the envy of his neighbours. 'Small wonder that all men tried to augment their income as best they could. In North Berwick it seemed as if the world stopped during the summer season. Golf dominated everything and the entire population seemed to be either playing or caddying. Building ceased and the fishermen took out their boats only at night. The pickings were rich. Boys were always needed and, at 1s. a round and 6d. for lunch, we thought we were millionaires.'

At weekends they would walk the three and a half miles to Muirfield, often caddying for two if not three rounds, and walking home again, the great day being Medal Day, when it was the custom of the gentlemen to pay the caddie 5s. One, Mr A. J. Balfour, who was to become Prime Minister in 1902, would stop his big, open car, the first that Sheridan had ever seen, and instruct his chauffeur, resplendent in leather breeches, jacket and goggles, to give the boys a ride home. Sheridan in his time at Sunningdale has never given a damn for anyone with red tabs, and the bigger the 'anyone', the more willingly they have generally taken it. The secret, we can now see, was absorbed at an early age from the eminent and Right Hon. Gentleman who gave him a lift nearly seventy years ago.

'For a kid of my age conversation with a Cabinet Minister was comparatively unimportant, but it was breathlessly thrilling to ride in a motor car when the mere sight of one ranked as a sensation. It may be that early contact with the country's rulers influenced my

subsequent attitude towards them. Certainly in my experience the
more elevated a man, the happier he feels to be treated as an equal.'

Mr Balfour, of course, was mainly to be seen at North Berwick and
helped to lay the foundation of the little town's reputation, which
lasted until the beginning of the last war, of being the place to be seen
in September. One is pleased to meet in real life in Sheridan's pages a
character legendary to my generation, the one-time professional, at
that time caddie and proprietor of the ginger beer stall at the 9th,
Big Harry Crawford.

'With his huge bulk and foghorn voice, Harry cut an awesome
figure, even to Mr Balfour. When the Minister collected any sweep-
stake money, he handed it over untouched to Crawford. A curious
affection developed between the two men. One a rough piece of Scots
granite, the other a cultured member of the Government. Harry was
in the habit of running up a flag on his stall whenever Mr Balfour was
on the course. It was his method of showing the respect he would
never put into words.'

Through one of those chance meetings that so often shape our ends
Sheridan was recommended by a friend at North Berwick, who had
been offered the job of caddie-master at Sunningdale but declined to
work on Sundays, to apply instead. He was taken on by Jack White—
one of only three men to win the Open with four rounds each lower
than the last—for a probationary period of six weeks and now, fifty-six
years later, he is waiting to know whether it is intended to confirm
his appointment on a permanent basis.

One of the great unpurchasable assets in a golf or any other club is
continuity of staff, and here Sunningdale has certainly been fortunate.
Another chance meeting brought Hugh MacLean south in 1898 to act
as foreman to Willie Park, who was to lay out the course. Until a few
years ago he still lived in his house in the middle of the course and now
his son, James, keeps on a family greenkeeping tradition that has lasted
more than sixty years.

Through taking a day off to watch the Lord Mayor's show, Bert
Chapman got the sack from his job, was taken on by MacLean at
double pay—4½d. an hour—and has now been about the place for sixty-
seven years. Wigmore retired from the locker-room after, I think,
forty-two years, while Sheridan's daughter, Anne, was asked by Guy
Bennett, the then secretary, to help with a few hours' typing and has
now been in the office for twenty-six years. An enviable record indeed.

Again, when Francis Ouimet, having defeated the British giants
Harry Vardon and Ted Ray in the play-off for the 1913 US Open,
came to play in a tournament at Sunningdale the following year
(he took nine at the first hole), his caddie was a small boy called Harry

Budd. During the round a spectator asked him who he was caddying for and after looking at the label on the bag he said, 'I don't really know, but I think it is a Mr Ointment.' Ouimet—in fact it is pronounced '*we met*'—'has been known to us,' says Sheridan, 'as Ointment ever since. And Harry Budd, fifty-three years later, is still one of my weekend caddies.'

When Willie Park sent for MacLean he took him to stay at the Station Hotel in what was then only a tiny village and after supper could not resist taking him up to show him the new project.

'They took a walk up the hill and into the inky blackness of the Berkshire countryside. Suddenly Park stopped and struck a match, which flickered briefly before dying in a few seconds. "There," he explained, "did you see it?" "What?" inquired Mac. "Sunningdale," replied Park, as if it were an invocation. "We can make this one of the greatest courses in the world." ' Most people will agree that they did.

It is amusing to reflect on the likely reaction of the caddies at Sunningdale today if ordered, as were Sheridan's sixty-five regulars in his early days, to 'parade at 8 a.m., rain or shine', spending the next hour raking bunkers, mowing the practice putting-green, cleaning up the surrounds of the clubhouse and doing odd jobs on the course. They were also responsible for running errands and for any small job which arose, but these duties brought no extra pay.

The pious founder of the Halford-Hewitt tournament had his leg pulled pretty unmercifully by Charterhouse teams before the war. Had they known that in the twenties he was known to the Sunningdale caddies as Mad Jack, his life would, I suspect, have been made virtually intolerable. 'He did everything at breakneck speed,' says Sheridan. 'He was always so anxious to reach the course that, before the train even stopped at Sunningdale station, he would shoulder his bag, leap out and tear up Ridge Mount Hill, reaching the clubhouse before any of the other cab-driven members.'

'Hal', it also appears, was a great club thrower, though later in life he became highly intolerant of anyone who threw a roll or meringue. The same Bert Chapman used to caddie for him and one day went at last on strike. 'I can't do it all, sir,' he said. 'Either you put back the divot and I'll get the club or you get the club and I'll put back the divot. I'm not doing both.'

Sheridan has remarkable felicity of expression. When he put his father's whisky in the poultry mash, he thinks the sight of 'a waddle of drunken ducks' the finest thing he ever saw. Of Harry Colt, the first secretary of Sunningdale, he says, 'Certainly the secretary had a fierce kick in him. But I prefer men like that. The others desert you when the wind blows.' Sheridan deserves a special award as the first caddie-master to add truly to the literature of golf.

PALMER 'CAN ALWAYS DIG DITCHES'

When I was a boy, golf was not really a respectable game for the young, and the thought that it would ever become so never entered my head. Now the Golf Foundation teaches so many boys and girls at so many schools that often when they grow up there is nowhere left for them to play. Almost overnight, so it seems, the game has become not only respectable for the young but the most popular pastime in the entire civilized world; and its heroes are the sporting idols of the millions.

The two greatest showmen in the game's history have indisputably been Walter Hagen and Arnold Palmer, but in what different climates they flourished, then and now. To attend, and probably win, the British Open Championship took Hagen about five weeks, including a short trip to Paris, possibly to win the French Open too. It cost him several hundred pounds; he enjoyed himself immensely—'call every woman Sugar and you can't go wrong'—and on one occasion had to borrow from his son, a chip off the old block, who had had a fortunate speculation on the ship's daily mileage, to pay the taxi on arrival back in New York.

Hagen probably made, and spent, twice as much money as any golfer up to his time and is widely credited as the originator of 'I never wanted to be a millionaire. I only wanted to live like one.' This he certainly did and, when he won the Open at Sandwich in 1928, he handed the first prize of £50 straight to old 'Skip' Daniels, his caddie. Like Palmer he had the most celebrated manager of his day, the late Bob Harlow, and in all their years together—again I believe, like Palmer and Mark McCormack—they never had a written contract of any kind. 'Harlow set up the dates,' Hagen has recorded. 'I played the tournaments and exhibitions and we carried the greenbacks away in an old suitcase.' His fee for an exhibition was $500. What he would have made today, when Palmer plays twenty-five exhibitions a year at $4,000 apiece, is anybody's guess.

I thought that after a long talk with McCormack some time ago I knew the ramifications of Palmer's extraordinary life and business ventures reasonably well, but an article by the former in the magazine *Golf World*—which I notice is taken from a book to be published in this country, and the sooner the better—shows that few of us on this side have any real appreciation of this fantastic phenomenon who has survived 'more than a decade of being written about, photographed, televized, filmed, exhibited, marketed, advertised, promoted, licensed and exposed more than any American athlete in history'.

McCormack's outline of fourteen consecutive days in Palmer's life leaves one with a mixture of feelings—admiration, incredulity and 'better him than me'. He buzzes all over the States in his jet aeroplane— 'an adjunct to his vocation, but you need only see his hands move delicately over the astonishing number of controls to appreciate that, like a golf club, here is an instrument which responds to him, one that he relishes making function to perfection. If Arnold were once again twenty-four and not sure what he wanted to do, I have no doubt that he would become a pilot.'

In these fourteen specimen days he has several sessions of posing for advertisements; he flies off to attend the opening of a food-processing plant built by his father-in-law (with whose daughter he eloped, much to the father's early chagrin and later satisfaction); he picks up four business tycoons 'as part of his association with the US Banknote Corporation' and gives them the treatment at his home club. He proceeds to Winchester, Kentucky, to play an exhibition match and be made a Kentucky colonel and, splendid thought, an Admiral of the Kentucky Waterways; then back for a couple of days with the heads of fourteen of his own Corporations, then off to a banquet in Toronto to launch his sportswear line in Canada. He spends another day working on his clubs—he has a thousand in the basement—trying to improve the design and reduce the processes in their manufacture.

In the same fortnight there occurs his thirty-seventh birthday, for which his wife has prepared a sort of 'This Is Your Life' surprise. The doorbell rings and she tells him to go and let in the man to mend the television. On the doorstep—wait for it!—are General and Mrs Eisenhower, bearing gifts and reporting for golf and dinner.

In the meantime he is called by the White House. General Ne Win, the Burmese strong man who only a year previously was contemptuously cutting off American aid and throwing out American businessmen, has suddenly decided to visit Washington. He is an avid ten-handicap golfer and President Johnson would be obliged if Palmer could come and meet him. Unfortunately, he has another exhibition match, whereupon the State Department accept his regrets and intimate that US relations would be much improved if he could schedule an exhibition tour to Thailand, Cambodia and Malaysia. All this in one fortnight!

What one likes so much about Palmer, apart from his inevitable courtesy and his ability to suffer fools and fans so gladly, is that he so genuinely loves the game of golf. Gary Player cannot wait to get back to his farm. Nicklaus likes to get away fishing. Palmer likes nothing better than to play golf. 'He has a deep affection for golf courses, a love of them, if you like. He wants courses to fight back at him and considers them gallant opponents. This attitude of cherishing the game and the elements of it is, for a variety of reasons, an unusual one in a touring pro. Most of them come to hate golf courses, in part because it is the course that thwarts their ambition and in part because they feel such an attitude is helpful to their game.'

What inference, if any, one may draw from it I do not know but it intrigues me that if McCormack wants to call Nicklaus he makes it between 10 and 10·30. Player is a 9 to 9·30 man—but if you want to call Palmer you do it sharp at 8·0.

I suppose that, though he certainly does not behave as such, Palmer is the wealthiest man in the history of sport, but McCormack finds it impossible really to convince him that he will never be poor again, that he is not only a millionaire today but will be for years to come even if he never hits another ball. He has main offices in five cities and corporations in countries all over the world—you can even walk down the street in Tokyo and see 'Tearoom Arnie'—but money to Palmer in his agreeably direct and simple way still means money in the hand or the savings account. Mortgages to him are something that banks foreclose on and come and take away the furniture. Alone, surely, among his countrymen his maxim is: 'If you can't pay on the nail, wait till you can.'

Even now McCormack cannot convince Palmer that he is secure for life. Sometimes when he has one of his losing runs he will look at his huge hands with the stubby fingers and will say, 'Mark, no matter what happens, I can always dig ditches.' Instinct tells me they would be positively the finest ditches ever dug.

HALF A MILLION WORDS OF GOLFING WISDOM

I had been meaning, 'by special request' as the actors say when they had intended to render an encore in any case, to write something about holiday golf, one of the first principles of which for the indifferent player performing on a strange course seems to me to be that there should always be 'somewhere to go': in other words, however short or elderly he or she may be, there must be no carry beyond his range without some alternative route. My mind went back to a society meeting on a well-known Surrey course where towards the end of the second round my partner, who was clearly not in the first flush of youth, began to be unable to carry the heather from the tee. Later he revealed that he was eighty-three and all concerned have looked at him with respectful admiration ever since.*

Instinct told me that this principle of having somewhere to go has been laid down by a somewhat superior authority to myself, none other than Bobby Jones, and on turning it up I found, 'The first purpose of any golf course should be to give pleasure, and that to the greatest possible number of players, without respect to their capabilities. As from the standpoint of the inexpert player, there is nothing so disheartening as the appearance of a carry that is beyond his best effort and that offers no alternative route.' This comes from the Master's pre-war half-million words of wisdom, sifted by that indefatigable editor, Charles Price, under the title of *Bobby Jones on Golf*. And, of course, once I got stuck into it, I forgot all about the specially requested treatise on holiday golf.

For the benefit of the young, and of such readers as have not yet woken to the gospel of golf, Bobby Jones won the British and American Open and Amateur Championships all in the same year, 1930, and at the age of twenty-eight retired from competitive golf but not from contributing to the game. Having turned 'businessman-golfer', he wrote two syndicated columns a week and made a series of films, incorporating such characters as W. C. Fields and Guy Kibbee, whom I would give a large sum to see again on TV, however late I had to stay up to do so.

The point about Jones is that he played 'modern' golf. You cannot compare Hogan or Palmer with Young Tom Morris: they simply aren't playing the same game. Jones was playing the same game and on the same courses, the only difference being that he had wooden shafts (if you have never played with one just try it and see!); he had a

* The late Sir Picton Bagge.

L

sharp-faced niblick instead of the broad-soled wedge with which even
I can guarantee to get down in three more, and often two, from a
bunker; and neither greens nor fairways, especially in America, had
reached the perfection to which they have been brought today.

Jones was perhaps the last of the very great total amateurs, in the
sense in which most of us use the term. In the eight years before his
retirement he won sixty-two per cent of the open or amateur
championships for which he entered in the United States or Britain.
Yet he would go for weeks on end without touching a club and, as
Price puts it, 'spent most of the tournament season playing incon-
sequential matches with his father and an assortment of cronies at
East Lake, his home club in Atlanta'. There were no more than three
months in the year in which he played in any tournaments at all, and it
is interesting to reflect in this ghastly jet age that to play in the Amateur
in California, where he was beaten in the first round by a young
'unknown' (in fact, Johnny Goodman, who a few years later won the
US Open and remains the last amateur to do so), Jones had to spend
the best part of four days each way in the train.

Price describes him as 'the most thoroughly intellectual golfer since
Harry Vardon, the Edwardian Englishman who practically invented
modern golf', and I am sure this is right. Now, alas, in the illest of
ill-health from a spinal malady—a case, if ever there was one, of the
Lord giving with one hand and taking away with the other—he
retains a perfect memory of the past and a lively up-to-date appreciation of the present. He thought out the game and his own methods
and mental approach with the greatest clarity. On the old adage, for
instance, of 'Never up, never in', which bears an implication of a most
obvious fallacy, he says, 'Of course, we never know but that the ball
which is on line and stops short would have holed out. But we do
know that the ball that ran past did not hole out.'

Sometimes in Jones's pre-war writings there is an unconscious echo
of 'Then and now'. On the art of 'staying alert' throughout a championship round, in other words never playing one of those disastrous
shots which have done the damage before you ever stopped to think
about them, he says that golf demands more continuous concentration
than any other game and emphasizes 'what it means, when playing a
first-class championship round, to concentrate upon the execution of
some seventy-two golf shots in a space of eighteen holes and over a
stretch of upward of three hours' time'. Upwards of three hours,
indeed! And now, doing the same scores that Jones did and on courses
only a couple of hundred yards longer, they take upwards of six!

Certainly golf can give you more sudden and more paralysing body
blows than any comparable game. Jones describes one which is new

to me and I pass it on because any golfer will imagine so vividly the feelings of his luckless opponent, Willie Macfarlane. It was in the first play-off after the 1925 US Open and at the fourteenth Jones was two shots behind. Macfarlane drove down the middle. Jones half-topped his drive and, slashing at his second with a spoon, sliced it into thick rough a hundred yards short of the green. Macfarlane pitched up to within fifteen feet, putting for a three. Whereupon Jones holed out for a three. The stricken Macfarlane, overshooting by a yard, missed the one back and instead of being either three or four strokes ahead with four to play was back to all square. Let us add, though, that he did hang on to the end and won on the second replay.

One of the main differences in American golf courses has been the tremendous watering of greens, which presents even the moderate player with 'target golf', like throwing at a damp dartboard. Now that more and more clubs over here are spending tens of thousands of pounds on automatic watering systems which 'pop up' in the night, it is interesting to read Jones's views before the war and only a few years ago. In the thirties he thought the watering was overdone in America and was 'in great measure responsible for the fact that tournament scoring is uniformly lower over here than on seaside links in the British Isles. The difference is attributable more to this factor than to the much-talked-of seaside gales, which, after all, do not blow constantly.'

Nowadays, he thinks there is no longer the wide difference between inland golf in America and seaside golf in Britain. Greens have become bigger in America and greenkeepers are no longer under such pressure to keep the turf on them in a permanently sodden condition. 'At the same time, it seems that turf conditions in Great Britain have come more nearly to approximate our own. On my visit to St Andrews with the Eisenhower Cup team in 1958, the main difference I noted in the Old Course was an increased lushness in the turf. Formerly, the fairways had been quite fast and the greens more than firm; such conditions made necessary a kind of maneuvering entirely unfamiliar to American players. Now the fairway turf has more depth and the greens are more holding. From this observation, confirmed by correspondence with some of my friends on the other side, I have come to suspect that British seaside golf as we used to know it no longer exists.' We have been warned.

Many of the great players of today spend hour after hour on the practice ground hitting ball after ball like white tracer bullets straight into the hands of their distant caddie. Rather typically, Jones had more 'amateur' ideas. 'The secret of beneficial practice is keeping a definite idea upon which to work. If you cannot think of some kink to iron out or some fault to correct, don't go out. And if there is a kink or a fault, as soon as it has been found and cured, stop immediately and don't take the risk of unearthing a new one. . . . A man cannot do worse than to practice simply because he has nothing else to do.'

What fun to sit back and dream of a world in which we would never again go out and practise, because we have 'no kink to iron out', or 'no fault to correct'!

THIS IS WHERE I CAME IN

By what slender chances does destiny shape our ends! The late and revered Bernard Darwin used to tell how, if his uncle had joined any other regiment, he would not have been posted to Liverpool and, if he had never been posted to Liverpool, he would not have taken his holiday in Aberdovey and therefore would not have laid out a golf course (with flowerpots for holes) and he, Bernardo, might never have been introduced to the game—and what a loss would then have been ours! Most people, I expect, could trace similar chains of circumstances and certainly I most distinctly can myself.

If, for instance, an uncle of mine had not sent his sons to the preparatory school of St Cyprians, Eastbourne, I should never have gone there myself, and, if it had not moved, before my time, from Carlisle Road to the site into which you slice your first drive out of bounds at Royal Eastbourne, I should never have sat, morning after sunny morning, gazing surreptitiously from the Greek Unseen at the golfers on the skyline, and with particular envy at the boys of about my own age who trailed behind them carrying their clubs. Living in rural Bedfordshire I might never have become conscious of golf at all—and then what a lot of fun and people and places I should have missed!

The school itself had a strong flavour of golf about it, since the headmaster, Mr L. C. V. Wilkes, was a pillar of the club, and scratch or thereabouts. His son, the Rev. J. C. V. Wilkes, one-time Warden of Radley, played for Oxford in the mid-twenties and J. C. V.'s son, J. V., for Oxford for the last two years. Life really revolved, however, round the figure of Mrs Wilkes, outstandingly the most memorable woman I ever met, whose death only last week at the age of ninety-one sent my mind back to what seems almost another world.

I last saw her only a year or so ago and she produced lists and photographs, remembering every one of whole generations of boys—the comparison with Mr Chips was irresistible—their names, their progeny and grand-progeny, or which war they were killed in. Suddenly she paused and said, 'You know, I really am beginning to feel my age a bit—now that my oldest Old Boy is seventy-five.'

She gave us a devil of a time sometimes, and life did tend to depend on whether or not you were 'in favour', but she was a wonderful teacher especially of history and English—and with it a pride in England which I scarcely like to mention, so highly out of fashion would it be today—and, as my distinguished colleague Cyril Connolly has written, 'we learnt with her as fast as fear could teach us'.

Many made their mark before falling out of the race; others are still running well. Poor George Orwell, for instance, whose *Nineteen*

Eighty-Four looks like coming true in the 1970s and who, if I may quote Connolly again, 'rejected not only the school but the war, the Empire, Kipling, Sussex and Character'. Or a pale, rather gangly boy, poor at games but fond of talking about riding. The Philistines called him Milksop Mildmay and, if his rein had not broken, he would have won the Grand National.

David Ogilvy, still very much with us, has singed the Americans' beards on Madison Avenue by creating an advertising agency whose clients' total turnover exceed the revenues of HM Government. He also 'created' Commander Whitehead, so that all good Americans now know what you mean by a gin and tonic. Before his time I once asked for one in a golf club in Detroit and only the assistant barman knew. 'I know what he wants. He wants a gin and queye-nine water.'

Ogilvy recalls that for suggesting that Napoleon was a Dutchman, on the ground that his brother was King of Holland, 'Mum' Wilkes sent him to bed without supper; and that, disliking a false emphasis in his opening speech in the *Comedy of Errors*, she 'seized me by the cheek and threw me to the ground'. Others survived to succeed in less prosaic spheres. I like to think, for instance, that I am one of the privileged few who remember Master Cecil Beaton's flute-like rendering of 'Tit Willow'.

If I have strayed from my proper subject in reminiscing about this truly remarkable woman, whom so many of our readers must have known and may remember with the same mixture of awe, affection and respect as myself, I may perhaps be forgiven. I return to the golf caddies, who set me going on the subject, and they, too, serve to resurrect a way of life that is gone, a world in which the word Discipline reared its now unfashionable head.

There used to hang on the wall of the billiard-room at Royal Eastbourne, and I hope still does, a document dated 1900 outlining their conditions of engagement and employment, and these, I am sure, had little changed by my day. The boys were paid 6s. a week and had to report every morning at 9.15 to Mr Fred Holly—whom I knew till the day of his retirement, after fifty-one years' service, in 1951. Most of the notice consisted of the scale of fines for ten sets of offences— and pretty intimidating they must have been, at six bob a week! Mr Holly booked the boys in turn, and, if you weren't there when your turn was called—'Missing Turn Through Want of Attention'— it was 1d. fine for every other boy sent out after your name had been called.

Throwing Stones; Fighting (I think Mr Holly must have turned many a blind eye here, for they always seemed to be wrestling and rolling on the grass); Using Obscene Language; Shouting; or Annoying Any Member or Visitor, were all 1s. a time. Other offences carried steeply graduated penalties which, adjusting the value of money, would leave a nasty hole in the pocket of many a caddie today. What about 1s. first offence, 2s. 6d. second, for each or any of: 'Laziness . . . Inattention . . . Rudeness, Incivility or Smoking While Carrying Clubs . . . or Asking for Gratuities'!

The most savage penalties, however—2s. 6d., 7s. 6d. and dismissal—were exacted, and constantly risked, for 'Entering the Grounds of Any School, or Any Woods or Plantations', and this meant the steep rough bank down into our playing-field which trapped so many a sliced tee-shot. We regarded such balls as our 'perks'—somewhat supported by Mr Wilkes, who confiscated a brand new blue-dot Silver King before I had bounced it more than a couple of times in the lavatory—but the caddies made constant forays, and running battles were liable to ensue, conducted under well-understood but far from welfare-state rules.

The school sergeant, who had once played in goal for Plymouth Argyle, took pot-shots at them with a ·22 from a window at a range of no more than 120 yards, without, so far as I remember, scoring an outer, while two who were apprehended were treated on a par with the more privileged boys in the school and soundly beaten by Mr Wilkes. No assistant master being on hand to take photographs of their posteriors,* the school remained open—to the eternal benefit, if not of all, at any rate of the great majority, including your humble correspondent.†

* A reference to the newspaper topic of the day, the closing down of an approved school through allegations and photographs by an assistant master of excessive punishment by the headmaster.

† A member of the Lindrick golf club, contemporary with me at St Cyprians, wrote: 'My brother emerged from five years as a prisoner-of-war sane and fit, due entirely, in his opinion, to this background training!'

THE GENIAL GIANT-KILLER

I like to think of the small boy sneaking furtively across the fairways of the Country Club, Brookline, Mass., sometime around the turn of the century, on his way to and from the little Putterham school-house, built in 1768. Occasionally his pace is accelerated by the greenkeeper, but the risk is worth it not only for the time it saves but also for the fact that he so often comes across a lost guttie ball in the rough. By 1900, when he was seven, he had enough to last him for years. The only trouble was that he had no club—and, while people readily abandoned lost balls, to find a lost club was another matter.

Eventually his elder brother, who was old enough to caddie at the Country Club, discovered that a Boston store would exchange a new club for three dozen old balls. Thus he acquired his first mashie and the pair of them played incessantly round a three-hole course in the cow pasture behind their humble home. A few surreptitious holes at the Country Club at five in the morning, again until driven off by the greenkeeper, and then at the age of thirteen he played his first real game—a mile-and-a-half walk to the tramline, three changes of tram, and nearly a mile to the public course, then fifty-four holes of golf. His name, as you may have guessed, was Francis Ouimet, and his death will have caused innumerable people, in this country as well as his own, to say, as I do, that he was just about the nicest, gentlest and most agreeable man they ever met.

Scarcely seven years after his first game he changed the course of golfing history. In 1913 his heart was set on winning the National Amateur in the following year, but the Open was to be played at the Country Club, so he entered. On the eve of the tournament he played a couple of practice rounds at the Wellesley Club and in both took 88—or twenty-two strokes more than the record he himself had set. Yet a few days later his name was known all over the world, and the golfing flame he lit has been sweeping the United States like an unquenchable prairie fire ever since.

After three rounds he had the impertinence to be level with the British giants, Vardon and Ray, which is equivalent to a nineteen-year-old youth of merely local reputation tieing with Nicklaus and Palmer today. They did not in those days send the leaders out last and it so happened, to add to the pressure, that Ray finished, in 79, just as Francis started and that he heard while he was playing the 5th that Vardon had tied with Ray.

He heard that Jim Barnes 'had it in his pocket'—then that Barnes had blown up; then that a player called Tellier had it in his pocket—and now he had blown up. Now he himself took 5 at the short 10th and overheard a spectator saying, 'Too bad. He's blown up.'

It riled him, just as a similar remark riled Gary Player when he was 7 down to Tony Lema in that remarkable match at Wentworth. He rallied, and with six holes to play needed two under par to tie. He thought he might possibly get the shots back with a 3 at the 13th and a 2 at the 16th. At the 13th he missed the green altogether—and holed his chip. At the 16th, far from getting a 2, he had to hole a nine-footer for a 3.

Behind the 17th huge crowds had collected, blocking the road, and, as Francis got down to his curly fifteen-foot putt, an impatient motorist kept up a constant tooting of his horn. The putt went bang in the middle, and, when asked afterwards, he confessed that, such was his concentration, he had not heard a sound—perhaps the first, and true, version of the oft-told story of Harry Vardon and/or Joyce Wethered in similar circumstances saying, 'What train?'

At last he was left with the golfer's nightmare, a four-foot putt to tie for the Open—which, he has recorded, 'I popped in'—and so there they were, the three of them, next morning in the pouring rain, drawing straws for the honour and Francis drawing the longest. As he saw the great crowd, he trembled and wondered what he would do, but his ten-year-old caddie, Eddie Lowery (now a prosperous West Coast motor dealer and until a few years ago a member of the USGA Executive Committee), carrying his eight clubs said, 'Be sure and keep your eye on the ball'—and all was well. At the 1st hole he once again had a four-foot putt and 'as I tapped it in, almost instantly any feeling of awe and excitement left me and I seemed to go into a coma'.

We may leave him in the coma and pause only for a glimpse of the great Ted Ray, who, like the P. G. Wodehouse character, 'never spared himself in his effort to do the ball a violent injury'. At the long 14th he was the only one who could get up in two and we may imagine him with felt hat pulled down against the rain and pipe jutting from his mouth.

'He put every bit of power into the shot but his timing was poor and he hit the ball far into a grove of chestnut trees,' and at the 17th, desperate now, he 'tried to cut the trees on the left and hit a prodigious wallop that cleared everything, but finished in the long grass'.

So, as they came to the end, the youth in the coma was three ahead of Vardon, seven ahead of Ray, and for the student of golfing psychology some rich moments follow. 'It did not enter my head that I was about to become Open Champion till I stroked my first putt within eight inches of the hole. Suddenly I became very nervous. . . .

A veil of something that seemed to have covered me dropped from round my head and shoulders. . . . I was terribly excited.'

His card was marked by our own Bernard Darwin and hangs in the Country Club today, where many a time I have gazed upon it with awe. For the ensuing years Francis Ouimet was our constant visitor as player, captain or camp-follower in Walker Cup matches, and in 1951 he was accorded perhaps the highest honour we have to offer, namely to become the first American captain of the Royal and Ancient Club.

It led to an extraordinary coincidence, and I remember no more emotional moment than at the dinner which followed his driving himself in as captain. Resplendent in his red coat, he had spoken for two or three minutes when suddenly he paused and, beaming genially through his glasses upon the assembled company, said: 'It may interest you to know, gentlemen, that it is thirty-eight years ago, *this day*, that I beat Vardon and Ray.'

GOLFING TREASURE-HOUSE OF THE WORLD

Having reached the time of life when one tends to repeat oneself, I cheerfully do so this morning in saying that we in this country or, to be more politically precise, we in the British Isles, have the luck to possess in our small islands the golfing treasure-house of the world. This is largely an accident of geography, for which we can take no credit but which has left us with an unparalleled variety of golf on heather and moors; on the Downs and in ancestral parks, complete with deer; and above all on those otherwise useless stretches of 'links-land' left by the receding of the sea anything up to fifteen million years ago.

We tend to think that this links-golf is the only 'real' golf and still obstinately play our Open Championship beside the sea. The more I travel, the more I think we are right, and the concentrated experience of the last fortnight confirms the opinion. This started with a visit to a new course outside Toronto, where they played the last of the four Carling world tournaments. It was a typical piece of North American golf architecture, with the gigantic greens which, I seem to detect, are becoming less and less popular, at any rate with the professionals. They consist of three or four distinct 'pin-positions', separated by huge slopes, and you tend to have either a chance of getting down in one putt or little chance of getting down in two. The green with which I was concerned on the television, though in fact moderately flat, measured fifty-seven yards from back to front.

This hole did, though, provide one memorable occurrence. It follows, in the form of a right-handed crescent, the curve of the Humber River, and we had numerous incidents of players going in or half-in the river, including Gary Player who played safe into it with an iron from the tee—surely one of the most mortifying strokes in golf—and lost the first prize of £12,500 by those two strokes. Little Chi-Chi Rodriguez, however, went one better. He sliced his drive completely over the river. The ball landed miraculously in a little clearing in the forest and the question arose as to whether it was out of bounds.

An official was summoned in an electric cart and one could see at a glance that, if it had been an opinion poll, he would have featured among the 'don't-knows'—for which one could hardly blame him.

His walkie-talkie having duly revealed that the opposite bank was still on club property, Rodriguez, who weighs 112 lb., was picked up bodily by his caddie—he happened to have drawn the biggest one in the tournament—and was carried across the river. The caddie then waded back for the 8-iron, the shot was duly played onto the green, and the player carried back, this time on the caddie's back like Blondin carrying his manager across the Niagara Falls—a tale which I must one day unfold in these columns. One thing was, of course, needed to complete the episode, namely that, after all this, Rodriguez should hole the putt for a birdie 3. This he duly did from about ten yards, and I am told it was the talk of half the golfers of America the next day.

That night I flew home to the usual nice, chilly, rainy morning at Prestwick, cursing aeroplanes for not flying either faster or slower and for depositing me at 4 a.m., long past my bedtime, only to be told it was 9 a.m. and one must now start a jolly new day. From thence onwards, in pursuit of a new series of BBC2 colour-filmed matches, I have been sampling one after another the golfing gems of the Old World, and how wonderful they are, more especially if you have witnessed, or are aware of, the golfing history that has been made upon them.

I do not go back far enough to have seen Cyrill Tolley holing that huge putt at Muirfield to beat Bob Gardner on the 19th for the Amateur, or Walter Hagen twice holing the course in 75 in a gale to win the Open in 1929, when only one man had a 74 all day. Nor, alas, was I there to see the Green Committee of the Honourable Company of Edinburgh Golfers, when Hagen had done a 67 in the second round, receiving the telegram from a wag on the Stock Exchange saying SUGGEST PLAY OFF BACK TEES FOR REMAINDER OF CHAMPIONSHIP; but I can see to this day the extraordinary spectacle of John de Forest winning the Amateur despite the strange golfing disease of 'getting stuck' and staring, mesmerized, at the ball, completely unable to move the club.

We moved on to Turnberry where, disappointed in the last series, we now had a wonderful view of Arran and the distant encircling arm of the Mull of Kintyre and the volcanic rock of Ailsa Craig, and its colony of gannets—'Aloof, pale-eyed birds,' to quote Jacquetta Hawkes, 'pressing their warm feathers against the once molten granite.'

So across on the steamer to Portrush and Ailsa Craig's twin eruption, the Giant's Causeway, which Dr Johnson in a surly mood told Boswell was 'worth seeing but not worth going to see'. Here I recaptured in the mind's eye Pam Barton winning the Ladies Championship—and the rude fellow shouting to an early competitor from one of the trams which used to run beside the links, 'Go on, Maggie, 'it it'—and Max Faulkner, with two rounds still to go on the morrow, autographing a ball 'Open Champion 1951', and with his hands a yard apart, like a lying fisherman, telling some admirers about his pencil-grip putter and saying, 'I shall never miss another of those.'

Thence across the border to Portmarnock, the great links strangely tamed by an unnatural absence of wind and, playing for us, the mighty-hitting young Dutchman, Martin Roesink, whose name you may yet see featuring in world golf. Some say that the greatest round of golf ever played was George Duncan's 74 in the first Irish Open here in 1927, when a Force-10 gale removed all the tents and not a single other man broke 80. For myself, I see Max MacCready beating Willie Turnesa and wild scenes of Republican enthusiasm at an Ulsterman's victory. And, as we played the 17th, here of course was the moment in my colleague Patrick Campbell's historic match against the redoubtable Irish International, Dr Billy O'Sullivan, when the stewards came out with the ropes and one of them said to Campbell, 'Bejasus, I never thought we'd be needing these for the likes of you.'

Having paid the hotel bill, a notable document in that it is made out to 'Mr Lighthouse', we have now arrived at Killarney, on the sort of day you pray for, so as to show the lakes and the mountains to the world in all their ever-changing colours. I can still point to the spot where the late Valentine, Viscount Castlerosse, to whose family Queen Elizabeth I allotted the Lakes of Killarney 'and all the fyshe therein', said, 'Do you think we could make a golf course here?' and I said, 'I think we could make the most beautiful course in the world.'

If it is not, perhaps, a great golf course, it is in my own experience the most wonderful place in which to play golf—but now the same Dr Billy—or the Young Doctor, as they still call him in Killarney, though he is almost as old as myself—has called for me; the boat is ready; and we are to go shooting duck on the lake. Life has been somewhat exacting this last week or two—but Killarney on a day like this is compensation indeed.

THE LONGEST GOLF HOLE EVER PLAYED

One of my most prized possessions is a series of bound volumes of the *Strand Magazine* dating from the Sherlock Holmes era—'a world where it is always 1895'. I generally have one by my bedside, and for some time have been reliving the month of July 1913. What a loss it was when the *Strand* expired some years ago! Here in this one issue we have the first full story from Captain Scott's journals, the first facsimile reproduction of his last message as he lay dying on his way back from the Pole and a picture, among many others, of him presiding over his birthday party at Cape Evans on 6 June 1911, almost indistinguishable from his son Peter today.

For good measure there is a new W. W. Jacobs story and the closing episode of *The Poison Belt* by Conan Doyle, where the world wakes up again after twenty-eight hours of coma, and from the window of Professor Challenger's 'Oxygen Room' the golfers of Crowborough, illustrated by Harry Rountree, are to be seen resuming their game as though nothing had happened.

What really caught my eye, however, was an article entitled 'Marathon Golf' by T. H. Oyler. He was one of a party of golfers living near Maidstone who had been enjoying a day's golf at Littlestone and were now waiting on the platform at Appledore Junction for a train to take them home. Their talk turned to freak golf matches and how many strokes would be needed by two players, hitting alternate shots, to get from Maidstone to the first green at Littlestone. Somebody suggested 2,000; a 'Popular Sporting Parson' said that he would lay a fiver against this proposition, and within a minute or so Mr Oyler and an unnamed partner had accepted the bet and settled the details.

They started, 'in the early morning of a beautiful day in spring', from the north gate of Squire Cornwallis's Linton Park, just south of Maidstone, each with brassie, cleek and niblick, plus 'about half a gallon of old balls which were newly painted and carried in a bag'. Mr Oyler teed up, but the Squire's carriage drive was of a 'snakelike form, its sinuous windings extending for some two or three hundred yards', and their opening stroke finished in a rhododendron bush, from which they had to pick out under penalty. So did their next, so they kept to the cleek till they reached the cricket ground and eventually, after several stymies by trees, a high niblick shot took them over the fence and into the pastures beyond. From this point those not above being amused by such simple activities may care to follow them on a map, for they have thirty-five miles yet to go.

They reached, but alas did not carry, the River Beult in 65, and at 11.25 a.m. arrived at Hertsfield Bridge with a good brassie shot

(No. 97), which carried both river and road. From here it was a question of hedging and pitching, mainly with the niblick, till Hawkenbury Bridge, just west of Headcorn, where shot No. 158 was driven onto the South Eastern and Chatham Railway, 'at the spot where many years ago a disastrous accident happened to the boat train in which Charles Dickens was a passenger'.

No. 213 brought them to Headcorn at 2.30, when they stuck a stump in the ground to mark the ball and retired to the village inn. On emerging, they found that their caddie had decamped—the first of seven to prove unable or unwilling to stay the course—and by six o'clock they stopped at Crampton House Farm between Biddenden and High Halden and called it a day.

Next morning their troubles began in earnest. They were chased off by a hostile farmer, the new caddie got into a fight with another boy and had to be sent home, and a cross wind made the going very tiring. They lost a stroke through moving the ball while addressing it and then came to a high fence which they hit five times before getting over. Having sliced into a hop garden and hacked out of a wood, they passed close to St Michael's church and Harbourne House and 'found some good brassie lies in a field of oats which had been quite recently rolled'. More woods loomed ahead, so they decided to bear left and make for Ingledon Park, which they entered with a fine brassie shot over the fence. It being their 500th stroke, they took an interval for refreshments and 'on resuming, several trees were hit'.

They had hoped to reach Appledore by 2.30, but what with dykes, ditches, the military canal (in which they lost a ball) and a detour round Tenterden, it was 4.25 by the time they retired to the village inn for a belated luncheon. What sort of luncheon you would get in a similar establishment at 4.25 today, fifty-four years later, is anybody's guess. However, they struck the railway hotel at Appledore with their 785th stroke, putted over the level-crossing and a mile or two later drove in their stump, walked to Brookland station and spent the second night at Lydd.

Next morning they were back among the dykes near Snargate, but a friend in the village of Brenzett fortified them with sloe gin, which greatly assisted their progress. They passed the old Norman church at New Romney and now the end was in sight, in the shape of the tall water tower at Littlestone. A ball was lost down a rabbit hole, but nothing could stop them now and at 11.38 on the third day they holed out in 1,087. After all this they had lost only seventeen of the original half-gallon of balls and had gained the Popular Sporting Parson's fiver by no fewer than 913 strokes.

WHEN IN DOUBT, RETIRE TO THE PUB

I find something indescribably comical about the luckless Scottish footballers being piously fined £250 apiece while their equally pugnacious conquerors get £2,000 and a motor car, even if it would be stretching their sense of humour a little to expect them to share this view.* Thoughts of 'holier-than-thou' were passing through my mind when it occurred to me that golf players are protected from potential bottle-throwers by ropes—just as members of the Irish Dail in Dublin are protected from a critical public by wire grilles. Furthermore, the present sweetness and light have not always prevailed in golf.

In 1855, for instance, when Willie Park and Tom Morris were playing the fifth of a series of six £100 challenge matches, refereed by the Edinburgh publisher Robert Chambers, feeling began to run high and partisan spectators continually interfered with Old Tom's ball. I trust that Scottish readers will not accuse me of provocation when I say that the match was at Musselburgh. At any rate things got so bad that Morris and Chambers sought sanctuary in a pub and refused to come out, whereupon Park sent in a message to say that he would play the remaining holes by himself and claim the match.

The two refugees, still deeming discretion to be the better part of valour, stayed put in the pub and were eventually held to have forfeited the stakes.

In more recent times the final scenes in the 1925 Open at Prestwick would, in football terms, have been sufficient to close the ground. Poor Macdonald Smith, the expatriate from Carnoustie long resident in America and one of the world's greatest swingers of a golf club, was poised at last to win the championship. Rounds of 76, 69, 76, had left him with a lead such that a mere 78 would have seen him home and colossal crowds turned out to see the Scotsman win. In their determination to see the play at all costs (or, in the case of those who did not pay to come in, no cost) they trampled their hero into a tragic 82 and lost him the ambition of a lifetime.

Golfers are liable to be harassed more by natural elements than

* This was after the final of the 1967 World Club Championship in Montevideo, when the Racing Club of Buenos Aires beat the Scottish club, Celtic. Fouls and fighting were incessant throughout the match, and six players were eventually sent off the field. The Scots were fined £250 each, thus saving the club £2,750 in wages, while the Racing Club of Buenos Aires, after giving each player £2,000 and a motor car, offered to give the cup back. The £250 fine was reckoned to bear hardly on the Scottish goalkeeper, who only came in as a reserve after the regular goalkeeper had been stunned by a stone, and took no part in the fighting!

human, and heroic deeds have been performed against the full forces of Nature. I mentioned the other day a recent visit to Portmarnock on the shores of Dublin Bay, where the scampi are meant to come from but, alas, mostly don't. It seemed almost eerie to find a day on which all the flags lay limp and lifeless with not a breath of wind to stir them, and I recalled in imagination the scene when George Duncan won the first Irish Open in 1927 with a final 74, often quoted as the greatest round of golf ever played. Mr J. F. S. Macnie, another Scottish ex-patriate, who was there at the time, writes vividly from Argentina.

'Even allowing for the mist of memory, I cannot believe that golf was ever played in worse conditions before or since. The gale drove the torrential rain horizontally across the course; hats disappeared; raincoats, oil-skins, all were quite useless; spectators, battered into a state of mindless terror that they themselves would go bowling away, lay down on the ground beside the greens, head or feet to wind, so that the water could flow past on either side.

'Like most, I followed Compston, the only player on the course in slacks, who was among the leaders starting the last round. None of us gave a thought to Duncan, who was miles behind. But watching Compston gave one, in retrospect, a measure of Duncan's achievement. Having seen what it was like out there, when Compston finished in 84 we all thought he had won; what's more we felt we had seen a splendid round of fighting golf in impossible conditions . . . scores of 90-odd were ten-a-penny, so when rumours began seeping back about the progress of Duncan's round blank disbelief was universal.

'Anyway, a few of us beat blindly into the wind and rain and found Duncan coming up to the 17th green in the midst of a small crowd of followers who had the dazed but exalted air of those who have wit-nessed a miracle. He galloped happily through the few remaining strokes of his round, grinning like a swarthy pirate as he carelessly missed putts of a yard on each of the last two greens. He knew he had won.' The 'swarthy pirate'—what a perfect description!—won in fact with a total of 312. The next year's winning score was by comparison twenty-four strokes lower.

Whatever the conditions at Portmarnock that day, they must surely have been equalled at Sandwich in 1938 as the most severe in which championship golf has been actually played, as against abandoned. This I myself remember, and with more satisfaction than most, since I won a sizeable sum on the winning total—295 against a Stock Exchange quotation of 283. After two rounds three players (John Busson, John Burton and W. J. Cox) were tied at 140, with no inkling of what was to come. Before play began on the last day the huge eight-masted exhibition tent, 300 feet by 60, had sunk with all hands; sweaters had

M

been blown onto the shore the other side of Prince's, and I distinctly
remember a steel-shafted club twisted grotesquely into a figure of eight.

It may be unworthy, but which one of us can deny a kind of morbid
delight in seeing the great men of golf taking an enormous number of
shots? Here was a positive feast: 9s, or even 10s, were hardly worth a
mention. One anonymous hero took 14 at the Canal hole: 3 out of
bounds into Prince's and playing 7 off the tee; in the rough in 8,
bunkered in 9, two shots in the bunker and out in 11, on in 12. This
saga of misfortunes ought, one would have thought, to end 'and
three putts, 15', but no. He got down in two more for his 14. Only
three players broke 80 twice that day—Reg Whitcombe, the winner,
James Adams and Henry Cotton. In the morning only nine broke 80,
in the afternoon, only seven. Best of the day was Cotton's final 74,
comparable surely with Duncan's at Portmarnock.

Nor are the mishaps of lesser men without their appeal. Only two
years ago there appeared for the qualifying rounds at Southport a
splendid character by the name of Walter Danecki, from Milwaukee.
He was a professional, he said, and was 'after the money'. After an
opening 108 at Hillside, he slipped to 113, making a total of 221—83
behind the leaders, and 81 over par. His second-round score, extremely
steady when you realize that he had no major disaster and only one 10,
will bring much comfort to the more humble golfer and deserves a
wider public, so here it is: 7, 7, 8, 5, 5, 7, 9, 5, 5—58; 9, 6, 10, 4, 6, 5, 5,
4, 6—55 — 113.

Our most persistently successful money-winner nowadays is Neil
Coles, but it was not, I see from the handbook, ever thus. In 1953 he
and his cousin John, seventeen and eighteen at the time, were trying
to qualify for the match-play championship at Dunstable Downs, a
course I know well, since I once socketed five out of six practice shots
into a chalk pit. John drove five balls out of bounds at the 1st and
opened with a 16. Neil on the shortest hole on the course was bunkered
in 2, took 10 to get out—'and three putts, 15'.

My own hard-luck story concerns a player called Sandow, who in
the first qualifying round for an Open Championship at Hoylake
took 91 and retired. Next day I played round to mark his partner's
card, eager to show that I might even have qualified myself. I opened
with a magnificent par-4 and a fine drive down the second. Then, as
better men have done before me, I hit the second shot a little thin and
it caught the bunker. Behind me were two lady spectators. 'Ah', said
one of them consulting her programme, 'that's Sandow. He took 91
yesterday.'

If there had been a pub handy I should instantly, like Old Tom, have
retired to it.

SOCKETERS CAUGHT SLIP AND COVER POINT

No item of golfing intelligence pleased me more on returning home from sunnier climes than that a member of the Davenport club in Cheshire had done a hole in one not with a 9-iron but with a 9-wood. He had been a victim, it seems, of socketing—indeed at this same hole, which is only 130 yards long, he had once socketed his way to an 11 when faced with a distant prospect of winning the club championship—and so, believing himself incurable, had ordered a complete set of woods down to the No. 9.

For such non-golfers as we hope may occasionally read these columns, I should add that a socket, or shank, is a stroke hit not off the face of the club but off the angle where the head joins the shaft, the result being that the ball shoots off with a pathetic click, often only knee high and almost at right angles to the intended line. It is the most demeaning shot in golf, perhaps in any game.

The extraordinary thing about it is that the victims, having rarely any idea how they do it, almost inevitably know when they are about to. Furthermore, such is the power of intersensory whatever-it-is that any one of four golfers, sizing up to a simple chip shot of, say, forty yards, knows suddenly that nothing can prevent him socketing it. At the same moment, without a word spoken, all three others know that he is going to socket it. Each of them knows that the others know and all three know that the victim himself knows that they know. A second later the deed is done and beautiful friendships have been lost through an untimely snigger at this poignant moment.

It is difficult all the same to remain solemn in a situation so palpably ridiculous as when, for instance, a grown and responsible citizen is endeavouring to run-up his third shot along a dead flat fairway on the first hole at Hoylake. Then a faint click, and the ball shoots at right-angles over the little bank and out of bounds. All four parties concerned, of which I was one—though not the striker—found later that it had never occurred to them that he was not going to socket out of bounds.

There is at Sandwich the legend of the late Captain P., who, well set to win the Gold Vase, socketed his third at the 18th hole and his fourth and his fifth and his sixth, until by now he had encircled the green and was round by the fence at the back. At this point, a broken man, he picked up and withdrew. It remained a painful subject and I was never quite senior enough to ask him whether at that critical moment he knew that he was doomed, but somehow I am sure that he did.

Many people quite seriously cannot bear to have the subject discussed in their presence. In *Bobby Jones on Golf* the great man says: 'Because the fear of shanking, by contracting the swing, induces shanking, the evil is cumulative, living upon itself. It is for this reason that I advise golfers who have never shanked to read no farther here. Shanking is a thing to cure, but not something to think about preventing.'

The players most likely to catch the disease, he thinks, are those who employ short backswings in which there is a minimum of hand- and wrist-movement. He once saw a man socket ten shots in the final of the State championship, and another in an Open actually socketed two with a putter! He believes that J. H. Taylor gave up for a year, so diabolically was he attacked by the malady. I have never heard of this. Does anyone know whether it is true?

The master socketer, or perhaps it should be socketeer, is W. J. Cox, and I may perhaps recall once again the incident when some of us were practising on the ladies course at Royal Lytham for the *Daily Telegraph* foursomes—and those prone to the disease had really better not read on.

One or two of us were watching Cox about forty yards away hitting pitch shots across our front, so to speak, when he looked up and said, 'Here you are. Catch!' and hit the most perfect socket, straight into our hands at cover point. 'Here's another. Lower down'—and this one flew straight to us knee high. He must have done at least a dozen—and just before going out to play!

We slunk away, afeared, but he remains to this day undismayed, on the principle of 'know thine enemy'. In other words, you need never socket if you know how to. In the public interest, with feelings akin to those of the missionary entering the leper colony, I invited him to show me how. Very simple. You merely aim to hit the ball with the bottom of the shaft. I tried this, pushing right outwards as the club came down to the ball, and am not making it up for the sake of a good story when I tell you that I hit a succession of shots so perfect that I remember them to this day. Determined to master it, I eventually took aim at a point on the far side of the ball, resolved to miss it altogether. At long last there came the sweet click of a really beautiful socket.

Cox is right, of course, in this being one way to socket, but the error one had to make in order to hit it with the bottom of the shaft seemed so grotesque that there must have been other ways. I have been looking up the masters and, if you want confusion really confounded, read on. Jones elsewhere calls it 'a failure to keep the left elbow close to the body when the ball is struck', the remedy being to 'brush the left trouser-leg with the left hand when you hit the ball'.

Archie Compston, in my opinion a great teacher though not everybody's cup of tea, said, 'I have never yet seen a socket that did not come from the right hand,' which he elaborated with 'they are nearly always caused by a sort of outward movement by the right hand, just at the critical moment'.

His cure was to 'eliminate the right hand and keep the action moving with the left'. George Duncan thought it came generally from having the left wrist locked: his cure—'to shove the club from the left shoulder and get the blade of the club open. You might also,' he said, 'be failing to bring the left heel back to the ground in time.'

Harry Vardon said that people often thought they were standing too far from the ball, and so reached out for it coming down. He added, significantly like Jones, 'If the left arm can be induced to caress the jacket all the way, the right arm cannot stray and the action is correct.'

Henry Cotton says it is caused by 'following through energetically before making contact with the ball . . . the right arm should straighten only after impact'. He goes on to say that 'a swing like a wooden doll— no wrist action—will at times effect a cure in the shorter shots'.

I could quote Hogan, Snead, Middlecoff, Boros and many another, but it will do to be going on with if you concentrate on caressing your jacket with the left arm, getting your left heel on the ground, eliminating the right hand, shoving the club from the shoulder, getting the blade open and pretending to be a wooden doll.

On the other hand the most sensational, incurable socketeer of my acquaintance—so much so that a couple of us the other day stood at forty-five degrees bending down as though catching them in the slips— looks in action exactly like a wooden doll. The truth is that it is not golf but a disease. When I introduced my friend to a fellow patient at the Brighton and Hove club they got off to some splendid exchanges on their common ailment, but the local exponent won hands down, I thought, when I overheard him saying, 'My dear fellow, I'm worse. *I'm a carrier!*'

SOCKETING—THE CURE AT LAST

Reverting to my comments on the dread golfing disease of socketing, which some people do in fact find so infectious that they cannot bear it to be mentioned in their presence, I hope to reply in due course to the innumerable letters enclosing miraculous cures, geometrical diagrams, assurances that there is no cure, and just plain sympathy. An Irish correspondent, declaring it in all seriousness to be a matter of 'major national importance', says that most sockets are not sockets at all and are in fact hit off the tip of the club. This may well be true of himself—he finished 14 down against bogey over eighteen holes but is now 'cured'—but is manifestly disproved for most of us by the 'mark of shame'—i.e., the white paint on the actual socket of the club, which is so hard to remove surreptitiously with the moistened finger and clings stubbornly till sandpaper can be applied at the end of the round.

From Wales it is proved with the aid of geometry that a socket comes from the right shoulder remaining elevated from the top of the swing and the left shoulder going up correspondingly higher—'thus unconsciously throwing the abdomen forward and thereby the forearms, too, in order to pass it'. I have a strong visual image of the master, W. J. Cox, socketing on purpose, and I distinctly see his right shoulder coming round and upwards but his left shoulder going down. His abdomen, like my own, needs no further movement, conscious or otherwise, to throw it forward.

Another correspondent, who lost his left arm in the war and claims the distinction of being 'possibly the worst of the regular playing members of the Society of One-Armed Golfers', confirms Cotton's theory that socketing is caused by a shortened backswing resulting in a hit with the right hand before the clubhead reaches the ball, in fact a 'snatch'. He can do it, he says, practically at will. A one-armed socket is indeed a sobering thought! This hero also plays snooker quite well but, alas, Joe Davis on watching him said, 'Looking at you has made me realize what is the matter with my short game. You snatch.'

My original friend who socketed out of bounds from forty yards short of the first green at Hoylake writes to say that, though the subject remains unmentionable and incurable, all is now well. 'The method is to use a putter from anything up to seventy yards short of the green. This at once does away with both socketing and "dunching". And even a well-topped one will very often find its way on to the green. For this reason I advocate the use of an old-fashioned aluminium-headed putter—the breadth of the sole is a great help in topping it well. After half an hour's practice the socketeer will find he can get amazingly

close to the hole either from the fairway, light rough or out of a
bunker.'

From the neighbouring Wallasey comes the tale of the man who
got a two at a short hole; chipped in for a two at the next, a par-4;
hit two fine wooden shots just short of the next—and then socketed
into a horse. 'Birdie, eagle, horse!' says my informant. Rather akin to
the anti-socketing advice of that doyen of Midland professionals, the
late Tom Williamson, of Hollinwell—'Use your h'arse, sir. Use your
h'arse.'

I was wondering last week whether it was true about the great J. H.
Taylor having once to give up altogether through socketing—and
with the very club of which he was the world's acknowledged master,
the mashie. The answer is that it is. Furthermore, the nameless fear
lasted a lifetime, for when Taylor was long past his playing days Mr
Robin Mays-Smith, of Rye, suffering from what J. H. called simply
'the scourge', went to see him at Mid-Surrey in search of a cure. He
refused to come out but dispatched an assistant instead. 'Don't let me
see you, Mr Robin,' he said. 'Don't let me see you.'

It is J. H.'s own son, Leslie, who confirms the tale of his giving up.
It was in 1908 and it got on his nerves to such an extent that he put his
clubs completely away for six months. He emerged to win the Open,
the French Open, and the Match-Play Championship, which was just
about all there was to be won in those days. So here, at last, is the cure
for socketing—six months' isolation. Taking each golfing ailment in
turn, I expect on this basis to be out of quarantine by about the spring
of 1996.

It is with mixed feelings that I admit to being so ancient that it was in the year 1930 that a number of us who played golf for Cambridge decided to band ourselves together and venture across to the land of prohibition and plenty, the United States. Those who could touch their fathers for £150 did so, while the less fortunate were provided for by the father of a member of the team, Billy Fiske, who already held the world record on the Cresta and whose name is commemorated in St Pauls as the first American to lose his life in the service of the RAF. With myself as the rather casual and I am afraid not very inspiring captain, ten of us set off in the good ship *Caronia*.

From the boat we went straight to the Huntington Valley Club, near Philadelphia, and experienced at once the 'sea legs' one had heard so much about. The ground seemed still to be moving and, no matter how slowly one swung the club, it never seemed to come down in the same arc twice. For me this had at any rate one beneficial after-effect, namely that I have never in my life criticized anyone who could not strike his best form immediately after crossing the Atlantic, even if it nowadays involves only sitting in an armchair and, presumably, 'air legs'.

Our match, and many of those to follow, was played by fourballs, which even then, I see, I described on my return as 'the prevailing, though iniquitous, custom in America', and we were duly beaten 4–1. It was our first experience of the huge, rolling greens which are also the prevailing, though not necessarily iniquitous, custom in America and, after Mildenhall, we could make little of them. The big moment came in the locker-room afterwards when my opponent said, 'I guess you boys would like a little drink.'

Awful warnings had been sounded before we left. It would be all right for them; they were used to it. Others talked of 'delayed action' and people dropping as though poleaxed. Many, it was said, went instantly blind from wood alcohol. I opted for gin and tonic and raised it with a lively surmise. It tasted exactly like gin and tonic, which in fact was what it was. Not always, however, were we to come out unscathed.

Our next port of call was none other than Pine Valley, beyond doubt in my own mind the greatest inland course in the world. Indeed, it made such an impression on me that before accompanying the Walker Cup team six years later I was able to leave behind a precise hole-by-hole description which proved exactly accurate except in one small detail. Here I played and was duly defeated by the great John Arthur Brown, still the presiding genius of the club and a regular performer in the spring and autumn meetings of the Royal and Ancient.

To be noticed by the Press naturally, we thought, added to our stature and I still possess references to us as the 'invading British collegiate linksmen' and even, let me tell you, 'famed stars from the dear Old Country'. We were taken, too, to an enormous banquet given by the City of Philadelphia for Commander Byrd, lately returned from remarkable exploits in the Antarctic, but my principal memory, I am afraid, is of the master of ceremonies announcing that only two pieces of music had ever been written for twelve women harpists and that the twelve women harpists he was about to introduce would play them both. The ladies came on draped in long classical robes and started to pluck at their strings but, alas, the clatter of knives and plates and the incessant chatter was such that eventually they rose in a body and swept out. I have thought ever since in terms of a 'sweep' of women harpists.

From Philadelphia we moved up to Boston, where we were at once knocked off, 8½–3½, by Harvard but, as we had been in a sleeping car all night and, furthermore, lost five matches by one hole, perhaps it wasn't bad. I do not imagine any university team would beat Harvard today, but I still believe we might have done it then. We then sallied forth to play a number of clubs, including the Country Club at Brookline, where I found myself matched against none other than Francis Ouimet, who on this same course had beaten Vardon and Ray in the play-off for the 1913 US Open. He beat me by one hole and, if only I could have saved a stroke or two here and there, I am convinced that he would still have beaten me by one hole.

We returned finally to New York and began playing a number of other hospitable clubs—which brings me to the peg on which my story hangs. One of these clubs was Mt Kisco, and here the members were kind enough to put us up in their homes. W. E. S. Bond, now a preparatory-school headmaster in Scotland, and I were billeted upon Mr and Mrs Donald Carr, for whom we formed a profound affection and respect. Donald Carr died some years ago, though not before going round the formidable Number Two course at Pinehurst in his age, namely 71.

His widow moved to England to be near her son, who is a member of Wentworth, and it was her death on Friday at the age of eighty that brought back to me these distant but still exciting days. A remarkable woman. Under her original name of Blanche Shoemaker Wagstaff she wrote, in verse, a charmingly simple life of Jesus, called *The Beloved Son*, the sales of which in America now exceed four million. Our long friendship survived, however, an ill-omened beginning, for Donald Carr in the goodness of his heart had 'acquired', in honour of our coming from England, a bottle of port. It tasted rather like ordinary public-house port but we smacked our lips appreciatively.

What was in it we shall never know, but in the morning neither of us was able to raise his head from the pillow, or indeed to move, let alone get up. Lest the boys or staff of Belmont House, Newton Mearns, should chance to read this, let me say that their present headmaster was by no means guilty of excess but only the victim of the real old-fashioned 'knock-out drop'.

Perhaps because we were mostly among the sort of people who had reliable bootleggers, this was the only occurrence of its kind. Nevertheless, it is salutary to have seen prohibition in action, to have seen leading citizens in the finest clubs in the land reduced to drinking furtively in the locker-room, and to have actually proceeded to an address with the classic instruction, 'Knock three times and ask for Charlie.'

In Camden, N.J. which we passed through on our day of arrival, a character had been warned by certain other characters that a 'pineapple' was liable to be cast through his window. Wondering where he should have his dinner, he decided the safest place to be a crowded restaurant. One may imagine, however, his feeling as his dinner drew to its close. As he came out, a black sedan motor car passed slowly by. The sidewalk echoed to the fire of machine-guns. After innumerable pictures, X marking the spot, and column after column on the victim's lurid past, the local newspaper account ended with the memorable words 'A bystander was also killed'. He never even got his name in the paper.

THE 'DOUBLE-DOUBLE'—31 IN A ROW

No one who was at Prestwick for the final of the Amateur Championship in 1934 is likely to forget the scene as a posse of burly, check-capped Scottish policemen escorted the equally burly young man in the grey sweater all the way in from the 5th green. This was Lawson Little, whose untimely death is now reported. His impact on British amateur golf, though not prolonged, was more effective even than that of Bobby Jones. His opponent at Prestwick was James Wallace, a lean, self-effacing Scottish artisan who on his way to the final had quietly removed no fewer than five Walker Cup players, British or American, but now he was forgotten, lost in the gigantic crowd which had turned out, and was still turning out, in the hope of seeing him win. The match had in fact been put forward an hour to enable Little to catch the boat back to America and at 2.20, when he won, people were still pouring in, some of them to their great aggravation actually paying to do so when the match was over.

Before coming on to Prestwick Little had already made his mark in the Walker Cup match at St Andrews, where he and Johnny Goodman had beaten Tolley and Wethered by 8 and 6 in the leading foursome and he himself had beaten Tolley by 7 and 5 in the singles. One expects an American to win the Amateur here in a Walker Cup year, and it clearly might just as well be Little as any of the others. When all was over, it was evident that it could hardly have been anyone else.

Five years previously in the 1929 Open, Walter Hagen had holed Muirfield in 67. Cotton's 67 and 65 at Sandwich in the 1934 Open—to say nothing of a 66 in the qualifying—were still a month or two away. It was fair to say, therefore, that Little's 66 in the opening round of the final set a new standard, certainly for amateur golf. I have been resurrecting the actual figures and, if you know Prestwick, it may be amusing to accompany him round again in the mind's eye.

If not, imagine playing a final against these figures on any course you care to think of:

4, 3, 3, 4, 3, 3, 5, 4, 4 — 33
4, 3, 5, 4, 3, 4, 3, 4, 3 — 33

This barrage left poor Wallace 12 down at lunch, and who shall wonder? Out they went again and it seemed possible that from twelve yards Little might take three putts at the 1st hole. Instead he holed it. The short 2nd was of course a 3. At the 3rd, or 'Cardinal', more than 500 yards and with a blind second, where he had had an eagle 3 in the morning, he now had a birdie 4. Another

big one went down for another birdie at the 4th and the short 5th
finished it—14 and 13. Against a par of 4, 3, 5, 4, 3 he had had 3, 3, 4, 3,
3. It gave him twelve 3s in twenty-three holes and a total of 10 under 4s.

Little returned to the US Amateur at the Country Club, Brookline,
and the Americans turned out in force to see whether a new star had
risen in their midst. It soon became clear that it had. There were six
rounds of eighteen holes and two of thirty-six and Little in fact never
let anyone get past the 16th.

He was an appallingly difficult man to play against. He was only of
medium height but his broad shoulders and barrel-like chest made
him in ordinary clothing appear almost as formidable as a padded-up
American footballer. His father was an Army medical colonel—so
that Lawson had been brought up with a certain amount of reserve
and was not at that time a natural mixer. He thought the game out
step-by-step and took his time about it, including deciding between
the five pitching wedges he carried among his twenty-two clubs.
Unlike some of the other mighty hitters of the day, such as Jimmy
Thomson, he managed to harness his great length. One cannonball
drive followed another down the middle till at last even the most
determined challengers buckled at the knees.

The experts tend to talk of a man being a good 'birdie putter', or
otherwise, and this is a point that all of us can appreciate, even in our
own less elevated sphere. In other words, do you reckon yourself
more likely to hole a ten-foot putt offensively to earn a bonus in the
shape of a birdie 3 or defensively to save a par 4? We are all one or the
other, and it is a matter largely of temperament. For myself, I admire
the qualities of the former but have always, alas, belonged to the latter.
By common consent Little was a great birdie putter. What with this
and his huge straight driving and his iron play remodelled on the
master himself, Tommy Armour, it was little wonder that they could
not beat him.

Little returned to defend his title at Lytham over yet another series
of nerve-racking eighteen-hole matches against opponents with
everything to gain and nothing to lose, and this time he did give them
one or two chances. The local hero, Tom Parker, should have had
him in the first round but let him off the hook, so there he was, once
again in the final, this time against that pillar of Midland golf and now
of the Seniors, Dr William Tweddell.

I did not see Tweddell win the championship eight years before,
but instinct tells me that this final must surely have been his finest hour.
He was, if it may be taken as a compliment and not as a reflection on
his opponent, the most completely 'amateur' amateur, a practising
medico with a golfing style to defy the textbooks. He stood with his

left foot far in front of the right, completely 'shut' and facing towards coverpoint. And then by a last-minute adjustment of the downswing he hit the ball fairly and squarely back to the bowler. When he got to the green he took out an aged long-headed wooden putter. Bearing in mind that he had entered largely because his own doctor had said that the fresh air would do him good, the odds against his beating Little over thirty-six holes at the end of a gruelling week could without offence have been quoted at 100–8.

Little, beating into the wind, won three of the first four holes and nearly the 5th, and was 3 up at lunch. Afterwards he faltered for a moment and Tweddell took the first two holes. Little rallied to go 3 up again but the Doctor, with a 2 at the 9th, a birdie 4 at the long 11th, and a 3 at the 12th, got them all back and now was standing over a twelve-footer on the 13th actually to go one ahead. It just failed, and so, at last, there they were on the 18th, with a colossal crowd dead silent and Tweddell standing this time over an eighteen-footer to square the match. But no. What a 37th it would have been!

To complete the story Little went back to America and, despite a young fellow called Rufus King, who at the age of fourteen had won an All-American trap-shooting tournament, firing four birdies at him in the first five holes, and despite being more than once 3 down, he held them all off again—champion on both sides of the Atlantic for two years in a row, the 'double-double'. To achieve this he had taken on all and sundry in the most exhausting form of golf to which a champion can be subjected, namely knock-out match-play—loser to pack his bag and depart—and had won thirty-one of these matches in a row, or, if you count his Walker Cup win over Cyril Tolley, thirty-two. It remains a record unlikely ever to be equalled, more especially as there is no longer any match-play golf in America.

So at the age of twenty-six there were no further worlds for Little as an amateur to conquer and he turned pro. To me, however, he never seemed quite at home as a professional—though this would not have applied today, when amateur golf is but a stepping-stone to a paying career. He did win the US Open in 1940, but even so, after the 'double-double', his career seemed something of an anticlimax. He won a number of other good tournaments, but as one writer has put it, 'by the time he finished celebrating, someone else had won the next one'. It is match-play that is the real guts of golf, and it is this that earned Lawson Little the respect with which he will always be remembered in Britain.

ANYONE KNOW THE FEELING?

One of the manifest absurdities of games-playing is the difficulty which besets golfers in propelling a ball 1·62 inches in diameter (or in future maybe 1·68 inches, but we will not go into all that again now!) into a hole 4¼ inches wide, across a surface specially prepared for the purpose—to say nothing of the extraordinary variety of methods and instruments they devise with which to do it. Indeed, the longest book ever written about golf would not fully exhaust the subject.

In modern times I personally should class Bobby Locke as the best putter, day in and day out, though other claimants would of course have their backers. In earlier days, however, there would have been no doubt about it. The answer would have been Willie Park, Jnr.

Willie was a member of the great Park family of Musselburgh. His father won the Championship Belt in its first year, 1860, and again in 1863 and 1866. The Belt having been appropriated by Young Tom Morris after his winning it three times running, the present Open Championship trophy was won by Willie's uncle, Mungo, in 1874 and by Father again in 1875. After a suitable interval Willie himself won it in 1887 and 1889 and when, five years later, the first English professional, J. H. Taylor, of Winchester, had the effontery to win the Open, Willie at once challenged him ('Scotsmen believed that a match provided the supreme test of golf') and beat him.

Those were the days, and I wish we could see them back—the days when there were none of these almost identical, if highly lucrative, seventy-two-hole stroke-play tournaments and when challenge matches were the order of the day. Park senior issued an open invitation to all comers for nine years, his challenge to play any man, especially Allan Robertson, appearing regularly in *Bell's Life*, now the *Sporting Life*. Willie junior also took on all and sundry, though in the nineties his services were so much in demand for designing and reconstructing courses that for long periods he hardly played at all. This was the time of the first great 'explosion' of golf from Scotland into England and across the United States, and among Willie's many creations were Sunningdale and the scene of the 1964 Curtis Cup match, Hot Springs, Virginia.

Nevertheless, his man-to-man record in the challenge matches was outstanding and was founded undoubtedly on his putting. He coined the phrase 'a man who can putt is a match for anyone', and its corollary 'a man who can't putt is no match for anyone'. In 1920, twenty-two years after Vardon had put an end to his challenge-match career, he produced a little book called *The Art of Putting*, a copy of which reaches me from a friend not encountered since we were reluctantly initiated into the mysteries of the Bofors gun on the same ghastly barracks square near Chester.

It really is excellent stuff. 'In it,' says the author modestly, 'I give all the knowledge that won for me the position of the best and most consistent putter in the world . . . I was uniformly successful and the great strength of my game was my ability to hole, with certainty, putts from two to three yards.'

At Musselburgh, and presumably elsewhere, the greens were 'not only as nature made them—often with ridges, known locally as "sows' backs"—but absolutely as nature kept them'. Along the ridges you were no good if you could not hold the ball on its line by a deliberate hook or slice and there is no doubt that the professionals of the day could do so at will, though whether it is physically possible with the present ball I do not know. I should like to see, though, what a man who could hook it into the hole along the side of a sow's back at Musselburgh could do on some of the billiard-table greens of today!

Willie Park writes lucidly and with the complete absence of doubt befitting the 'most consistent putter in the world'. He tells us clearly what we are to do, rather than what we are not to do. He knows the secret, and here it is. Some of it may be discounted through the difference in not only the greens, but the ball. 'It is a bad thing,' for instance, 'to change about from a heavy ball to a light one or vice versa, and equally bad to change from a large one to a small one, or from a hard one to a soft one.' Much of his advice, however, through its decisive simplicity could still bring salvation to sufferers today.

Park used a slightly lofted, shallow-faced, wry-necked putter with a long shaft, designed after long trial and error by himself and popularly known as 'Willie Park's goose-necked putter'. The loft was useful for 'cuppy' lies—none to be found, we may be sure, at Sunningdale today—but when you were lying well the goose-neck and the loft each had notable advantages. The bend in the neck made the stroke 'more of a pull than a push. It is much easier to pull the ball into the hole than to push it in.' This, incidentally, is exactly the feeling I have when playing with the goose-necked 'Crookshank' wooden clubs.

The loft enabled the player to stand nearer the hole and more in front of the ball, thus helping him to blot out the hole from view. 'My eyes are so steadily on the ball that I blot the hole entirely out of my sight. I never see the hole when I finally settle to hit the ball . . . I never look up until I think the ball has had more than time to get into the hole.' (And by almost the same post I had a letter declaring that the only way to hole short putts was to blot out the ball and look fixedly at the hole!)

The experts, however, show a remarkable similarity over the years. One of Bobby Locke's great secrets was to hit the ball, and only the ball; not 'lightly brushing the grass', as so many of the textbooks recommend. Says Willie Park, the demon putter of the eighties, 'I keep the club just clear of the ground. I hit only the ball, never the ball and the ground, and by keeping the club clear of the ground I hit the ball high on its centre, thus making it keep close to the ground on its way to the hole.'

I had thought Bob Rosburg, the American, who once did a 62 with nineteen putts in eighteen holes, to be the original 'tap', or 'pop', putter—as against the long, flowing swing of the textbooks. This short-and-sharp method is now widely practised—if only because few people can produce a slow, flowing swing when putting for $100,000—but eighty years ago Park too reckoned, for a holing-out putt, to take the putter back no more than about three inches, and then 'the club should be stopped decisively when it has described an arc of about six inches after hitting the ball'.

Henry Cotton was once criticized for ungallantly declining to crank the car of a stranded lady motorist when on the way to a tournament, on the ground that a single backfire might destroy his entire capital assets. 'The player should take care before an important match,' says Park, 'not to do any hard work with the arms such as using dumb-bells, etcetera. Even the carrying of a bag before play may spoil the touch. . . .'

He stood with his left foot completely withdrawn and the ball only five inches from, and just in front of, his right toe, and he held the club right at the bottom of the grip, crouching over the ball and using only his wrists. 'Players unaccustomed to stooping,' he says, 'feel a sensation of blood rushing to the head, and to eradicate this weakness should practise putting in the stooping position for at least three minutes before straightening up.'

Furthermore, he himself practised for hours on his private lawn with six holes, each only $3\frac{1}{2}$ inches wide—after which the real hole, he says, 'had the appearance of a wash-tub'.

Blood rushing to the head, and the hole only $3\frac{1}{2}$ inches wide! Anyone know the feeling?